The Media Manifesto

T0044897

The Manifesto Series

David Buckingham, *The Media Education Manifesto*

Natalie Fenton, Des Freedman, Justin Schlosberg and Lina Dencik, *The Media Manifesto*

Silvio Waisbord, *The Communication Manifesto*

Natalie Fenton
Des Freedman
Justin Schlosberg
Lina Dencik

The Media Manifesto

polity

First published in 2020 by Polity Press

Polity Press
65 Bridge Street
Cambridge CB2 1UR, UK

Polity Press
101 Station Landing
Suite 300
Medford, MA 02155, USA

ISBN-13: 978-1-5095-3805-8 (hardback)
ISBN-13: 978-1-5095-3806-5 (paperback)

A catalogue record for this book is available from the British Library.

Library of Congress Cataloging-in-Publication Data

Names: Fenton, Natalie, author. | Freedman, Des, 1962- author. |
    Schlosberg, Justin, author. | Dencik, Lina, author.
Title: The media manifesto / Natalie Fenton, Des Freedman, Justin
    Schlosberg & Lina Dencik.
Description: Cambridge ; Medford, MA : Polity, 2020. | Series: The
    manifesto series | Includes bibliographical references. | Summary: "Why
    there can be no meaningful democracy without media reform"-- Provided by
    publisher.
Identifiers: LCCN 2020002629 (print) | LCCN 2020002630 (ebook) | ISBN
    9781509538058 (hardback) | ISBN 9781509538065 (paperback) | ISBN
    9781509538072 (epub)
Subjects: LCSH: Mass media--Social aspects. | Mass media--Political
    aspects. | Mass media--Moral and ethical aspects. | Power (Social
    sciences)
Classification: LCC P95.54 .F46 2020 (print) | LCC P95.54 (ebook) | DDC
    302.23--dc23
LC record available at https://lccn.loc.gov/2020002629
LC ebook record available at https://lccn.loc.gov/2020002630

Typeset in 11 on 15 Sabon by
Servis Filmsetting Ltd, Stockport, Cheshire
Printed and bound in Great Britain by CPI Group (UK) Ltd, Croydon

For further information on Polity, visit our website: politybooks.com

Contents

Acknowledgements   vi

1 Challenging Media Power Today   1
2 Claiming Media Justice   26
3 Advancing Data Justice   48
4 Articulating a Politics of Hope   75
5 Conclusion: A Manifesto for Media
   Reform   100

Notes   118

Acknowledgements

This book is born of the media reform movement and owes its inspiration, ideas and arguments to the many activists around the world who give their time and energy to make our media worlds democratic, fairer, more representative, plural, diverse accountable and just. In particular we have drawn inspiration from Vanessa Baird, Steve Barnett, Laura Basu, Mike Berry, Ben Birkinbine, Benedetta Brevini, Brian Cathcart, Sasha Costanza-Chock, Kate Coyer, Malkia Cyril, Simon Dawes, Seeta Peña Gangadharan, Rodrigo Gomez, Bob Hackett, Dan Hind, Becky Lentz, Bob McChesney, Martin Moore, Graham Murdock, Victor Pickard, Nathan Schneider, Trebor Scholz, Hilary Wainwright and Todd Wolfson.

Each of the authors is also part of the Media Reform Coalition (MRC) in the UK. Since 2011,

Acknowledgements

the MRC has been at the forefront of the UK's progressive media reform movement, producing evidence and giving testimony to a broad range of public inquiries into the media; engaging the public on media reform issues; and designing innovative solutions that address the most critical issues in media policy-making: supporting media pluralism, defending ethical journalism and maximizing the public interest in media and communications. The MRC is made up civil society groups, academics and campaigners whose energy and commitment to media democracy runs throughout this book. In particular, we would like to thank members of the Co-ordinating Committee of the MRC who regularly give up their time to advancing media justice, and who have informed and influenced many of the ideas in this book. They include James Curran (Goldsmiths); Maggie Chao (38 Degrees); Sarah Kavanagh (National Union of Journalists); Jonathan Hardy (University of East London and formerly Campaign for Press and Broadcasting Freedom); Gareth Lowe (UNITE trade union); Riaz Meer (BECTU trade union); Kerry-Ann Mendoza (The Canary); Tom Mills (Aston University); Angela Phillips (Goldsmiths); Nathan Sparkes (Hacked Off); Damian Tambini (London School of Economics); Einar Thorsen

Acknowledgements

(Bournemouth University); Leo Watkins (Formerly Enders Analysis); Henna Zamurd-Butt (formerly Media Diversified); and Alaphia Zoyab (Avaaz).

The authors also share a common history in that all have at some point been part of Goldsmiths, University of London in the Department of Media, Communications and Cultural Studies. Goldsmiths deserves a mention for still being an academic environment where public and political engagement is rife and in particular for supporting the work of the MRC.

This manifesto builds on extensive academic research by the authors that has been carried out in constant dialogue with a range of publics, politicians, news professionals, journalists, activists, policy-makers and, of course, each other. While our ideas have grown together and we are keen for this book to be seen as a collaborative manifesto, we have each taken prime responsibility for the main writing of one chapter: Chapter 1 (Des Freedman); Chapter 2 (Justin Schlosberg); Chapter 3 (Lina Dencik); Chapter 4 (Natalie Fenton) and Chapter 5 (all of us).

And finally we would like to extend our heartfelt thanks to our wonderful friends and family, who have had to endure our absences as we take part

Acknowledgements

in endless meetings, rallies, conferences, festivals and assemblies, when engaged in the hard grind of political campaigning and trying to make good our manifesto wishes.

1

Challenging Media Power Today

Why a manifesto?

This is a time for manifestos: analyses that identify the faults and fissures of a divided world and declarations that propose strategies to put things right. We need narratives that articulate our rage against injustice and simultaneously evoke a spirit of optimism and the possibility of radical social change. This is not a time for studied neutrality, strategic ambivalence or cool indifference but an opportunity to diagnose problems and mobilize solutions.

The dominant neoliberal order has been widely discredited and its zombie form stumbles on, albeit with fewer and fewer supporters. Inequality and instability, discrimination and disillusion are rampant across much of the world and environmental disaster lurches ever closer. Public life has been hollowed out – increasingly administered by private companies and opportunistic elites in thrall to a blinkered market logic – while the dream of a digital nirvana appears to have turned into a cesspit of racist abuse, corporate surveillance and global bickering. Our universities are debt machines, our welfare systems are increasingly emaciated, and our systems of government are opaque to populations for whom direct democracy exists largely as a fairytale from Athenian times.

In response to the breakdown of what was always a fragile political consensus, we are now seeing worrying levels of nativism and xenophobia dressed up as 'popular sentiment'. Authoritarianism – marked by states of emergency, pervasive surveillance regimes and intolerance towards minorities – is by no means a tendency confined to distant 'illiberal' states but finds an expression in traditional 'liberal democratic' nations. Walls, borders, profits and privileges preoccupy vested interests far beyond any meaningful commitment to diversity, equality, climate action and social justice.

Our communication systems are not exempt from these developments. In fact they are crucial vehicles through which misinformation, misrepresentation, misogyny and mischief are disseminated. For example, Ogilvy, one of the world's largest and most prestigious advertising agencies, was happy to take $39 million from the American government in order to make commercials for US Customs and Border Protection at a time when it was forcibly separating children from their parents at the US–Mexico border and holding them in cages. Its CEO defended the agency's actions by pointing out that CBP 'is not necessarily a bad organization' and that, in any case, Ogilvy had previously worked with other controversial companies like BP, big tobacco and Coca Cola.[1] Moreover, the failure to predict, challenge or to make sense of apparently unprecedented events such as the election of Donald Trump, Brexit, climate catastrophe and the rise of the far right can't be blamed solely on fringe purveyors of 'fake news' but reflects the insulation, complacency and commercial interests of our major legacy news organizations. As the then CEO of US network CBS famously put it during Trump's 2016 presidential campaign: 'It may not be good for America, but it's damn good for CBS . . . The money's rolling in and this is fun.'[2]

Presided over by unaccountable oligopolies fostering corporate-friendly agendas and deploying algorithms whose operations remain shrouded in mystery, our news media are in thrall to the very power that they once promised to challenge.

Newsrooms now operate with fewer staff working across more platforms, desperately seeking the clicks and likes that will justify their wages, no matter whether this journalism serves the public interest or not. Meanwhile, giant media and tech companies who are either flush with cash (as of mid-2019, Apple and Alphabet alone had some $219 billion of cash holdings),[3] or who are heavily indebted (like Netflix, Comcast and Disney), are splashing out enormous amounts of money to generate new content and make strategic acquisitions in order to squash their competition and accrue yet more power.

The US politician Bernie Sanders makes an important point when he argues that when 'we have had real journalism, we have seen crimes like Watergate exposed and confronted, leading to anti-corruption reforms. When we have lacked real journalism, we have seen crimes like mortgage fraud go unnoticed and unpunished.'[4] Yet this inability to hold power to account shouldn't be seen as an unprecedented 'failure' of the media to perform its democratic role when, in fact, this has long been the media's normal role under capitalism: to naturalize and legitimize existing and unequal social relations. It's not about failing to hold banks to account but about the complicity of financial journalists and commentators in celebrating neoliberal economics ahead of the 2008 financial crash; it's not about failing to be tough on racism but about the media's historic perpetuation of racist stereotypes and promotion of anti-immigrant frames; it's not about failing to recognize the challenges of apocalyptic climate change but about repeating tropes about 'natural' disasters such as hurricanes, heatwaves and forest fires, together with routine 'balanced' debates between climate change scientists and deniers. These are not examples of the media's malfunctioning but of its default behaviour.

We need, therefore, to promote a different kind of media as a fundamental feature of a different kind of social system. Fortunately, the rising tide of racism and authoritarianism coincides and clashes with an appetite for collectivist approaches and an embrace of social justice. Despair and defeatism about current trends of polarization and illiberalism is matched by a growing enthusiasm for more radical and progressive solutions.

In this contradictory and volatile context, what form of writing is better placed to host imaginative and activist critique than the not-so-humble manifesto, the choice of groundbreakers, revolutionaries and iconoclasts for over 500 years? Left political movements, artistic currents, anti-colonial struggles and liberation campaigns have both used and, in part, been constituted by manifestos that proudly declare their provenance. Communism, nationalism, feminism, anti-colonialism, surrealism, dadaism, futurism, vorticism, situationism, slow tech and open access have all used the manifesto form as a launchpad and weapon of choice.

As with any manifesto, ours combines analysis and advocacy, critical theory and a call to action. The book analyses the pitfalls and priorities of contemporary media and tech in the context of our determination to secure a future based on the redistribution of society's resources, in order to secure political and economic equality. It outlines the contours of an expansive media power in contrast to the fragmented and distributed character with which it is often associated; it explores the dangers of a dependence on data and highlights key myths that underpin today's media and tech policymaking; and, crucially, it proposes a programme of media and data justice based on the identification of a 'politics of hope' that is itself inspired by emerging social movements and counter-hegemonic projects. As with any manifesto, its value can only be understood in relation to the solidarities it fosters, the energy it encapsulates and the change it promotes.

The triumph of executive power

Politicians, scholars and publics are all preoccupied with the media because they are seen to have enormous influence and power. But what is the nature of this influence and what does 'media power' actually mean? Does it refer to ability of major platforms and outlets to shape agendas and disseminate content in line with their own interests? Does it refer to the subtle ways in which some representations and narratives are normalized and others discredited? Does it refer to the control of a society's symbolic resources and, in the words of the French sociologist Pierre Bourdieu, the capacity to 'construct reality' in line with dominant assumptions and to secure a 'consensus which contributes fundamentally to the reproduction of the social order'?[5] Is media power a property dominated by billionaire moguls and giant corporations, or a capacity distributed more generally and experienced more intimately to 'make meaning' and to cement identities? To what extent, to paraphrase an old sociological dilemma, does media power contribute to the domination of certain groups over others, or is it rather a means through which societies come to know themselves and share collective representations?

This book argues that media power constitutes a

central way in which social norms are proposed and policed by elite interests and that it is a regulatory force committed to upholding a status quo based on private property and the rule of capital. While it is not immune from the contradictions and tensions that are to be found in all societies[6] – indeed the most effective forms of media power are precisely those that provide limited expressions of discontent within a more general embrace of existing social relations – its loyalty is to a capitalist logic in which it is deeply embedded. Tech owners, newspaper editors, senior broadcasters, advertising executives, regulators and policy-makers are all partners – even if, at times, warring ones – in the management of media markets and systems across the globe. Their power is vested in economic and political control of communications landscapes – a dominance that is scarcely comparable to the far more limited opportunities for individuals to deploy their own symbolic resources.

Yet the cry from media moguls and some media theorists is that this is an outdated picture of a consolidated and concerted media power; one that perhaps fitted the monopoly conditions of a former analogue century but certainly not the heterogeneous character of the digital present. 'Haven't you heard of the Internet? No one controls the media or will ever again', tweeted Rupert Murdoch back in 2012.[7] Media power is now said to be more fragmented, dispersed, opaque, complex and polycentric in the light of digital transformations, the falling cost of entry to media production and distribution, the decline of traditional media and the more general dissipation of expertise and authority. Media are no longer 'sticky' but 'spreadable'[8] and analysis of media power should be liberated from its functionalist and conspiratorial associations with top-down forms of control. According to one influential theorist, media power should be understood 'in a non-reductive and multifaceted sense, as the use of resources, of varying kinds, that . . . enable individuals or collectivities to pursue their values and interests'.[9]

That media power can now be seen as productive and *not* disabling owes much, of course, to the legacy of Michel Foucault and his proposition, developed throughout the 1970s, that power is not always 'prohibitive' but resolutely constitutive of human subjectivity. In one very famous expression, he declares the following:

> We must cease once and for all to describe the effects of power in negative terms: it 'excludes', it 'represses', it 'censors', it 'abstracts', it 'masks', it

9

'conceals'. In fact power produces; it produces realities; it produces domains of objects and rituals of truth.[10]

Foucault isn't arguing that power is simply a benevolent or equalizing force but he is anxious to disentangle power from a single source of domination – such as class or wealth – and instead to paint it as a far more amorphous, if ubiquitous, phenomenon. Power is now to be understood as a 'machine in which everyone is caught, those who exercise power just as much as those over whom it is exercised'.[11] In a decisive shift away from power being the tangible property of a specific social group, Foucault encourages us to think in terms of 'capillary power', 'biopower', 'pastoral power' and 'panoptic power' – all of which highlight the role of dispersed and self-policing individuals in the production and reproduction of power.[12]

Despite the ongoing resistance emanating from critical political economists of the media and stubborn Marxists, the idea that power seeps, drains and circulates effortlessly throughout society – that it operates without an overarching class dynamic – remains pervasive.[13] While this approach has expanded our vocabulary and highlighted experiences perhaps marginalized by more singular perspectives, it has sidetracked our politics by encouraging us to look away from those sites in which power remains highly concentrated. These include the state, which continues to shape the dynamics of the communications landscape, and capitalist firms, which exert an increasingly tight grip over sectoral media markets, as well as influencers (from presidents to commentators to celebrities), whose voices are amplified by gatekeepers hungry for traffic. In this situation, the most effective metaphor for media power is no longer the panopticon but the watch tower, not the network but the hierarchy, not entrepreneurial pebbles but industrial boulders, not the long tail but the blockbuster.

This points to a context in which we face the challenge of a renewed *executive power* where elite groups deploy their resources – their access to capital, their political influence and their ideological congruence – to dominate contemporary media systems. Karl Marx wrote about the triumph of executive power over legislative power in relation to mid-nineteenth century France in *The 18th Brumaire of Louis Bonaparte*. He described its 'enormous bureaucratic and military organization with its wide-ranging and ingenious state machinery' and condemned 'this terrifying parasitic body which enmeshes the body of French society and chokes all its pores'.[14] Of course, the context is radically different some 170 years on but are we really in a situation in which we are free of instrumental calculations, imperial ambitions, state machinations and complicit relationships when we think of the role of, for example, Google and Globo, Fox and Facebook? Indeed, social media algorithms, state surveillance systems and a 'club culture' at the top of the media would suggest that this form of power is more deeply embedded than ever.

Executive power is not counterposed to the more individualized character of self-governance but actually creates the conditions and sets the parameters for these intimate flows of power. For too long, however, media and cultural theorists have been preoccupied with a microphysics of power at the expense of naming, shaming and opposing the key institutions and individuals that hegemonize the media: tax-avoiding corporations and offshore billionaires; data brokers and infrastructure empires; market-friendly politicians and captive regulators; complacent commentators and establishment editors. These are the neoliberal vanguards who preside over media and communications in defence of a status quo that suits their material interests and it is in their shadow that this manifesto sets out its stall.

Executive media power on trial

The hope that patterns of concentrated power in legacy press and broadcasting markets would not be replicated in digital conditions has long since evaporated. Now there are regular warnings about the dangers of an oligopolistic tech sector that, thanks to lax (or nonexistent) regulation and an avaricious DNA, is accruing a massive amount of power and undermining the conditions for a deliberative democracy. Facebook, as Siva Vaidhyanathan argues, is both a 'pleasure machine' and a 'surveillance machine', a 'protest machine' and a disinformation machine' that is structurally fixated on hoovering up personal data and circulating content no matter its accuracy or consequence.[15] Together with Google, it is expected to account for just under 65 per cent of all digital advertising in the UK and 59 per cent in the US by 2021. Google alone earns more from advertising than the ad revenue of China and the UK combined; indeed Google's ad revenue is larger than that of any ad market in the world with the exception of the US.[16] We are truly in an age of 'digital dominance' manifested by growing public concern with 'user autonomy, user agency and the power of platforms to impact the decision-making of consumers and citizens through profiling, information control, and behavioural nudges'.[17]

Yet the size and impact of these digital behemoths should not distract us from the continuing presence and impact of legacy media that are reconsolidating precisely in order to face up to digital challenges. Today's global media giants include not only the FAANG companies (together with their Chinese counterparts, Alibaba and Tencent) but household names from across the world including Sony, Disney, Comcast, Bertelsmann, Televisa and Prisa.[18] In the US, where Disney controls more than 40 per cent of Hollywood box office and accounts for some 30 per cent of all primetime scripted broadcast programmes, a wave of mergers is taking place to better allow 'traditional' media to compete in digital media markets.[19] In Brazil, Grupo Globo is dominant across all media sectors and boasts that it reaches over 100 million Brazilians, some 50 per cent of the population, every day. In Argentina, just four conglomerates have nearly half of total audience share across television, radio, print and online, with the Clarin Group alone accounting for 25 per cent of consumption. Media markets across the globe are characterized by oligopolistic structures and cartel-like behaviour.[20]

Public policy, however, is increasingly gripped by

the threat of digital disinformation (as we discuss further in Chapter 4) and the need, above all, to regulate and to 'rein in' out-of-control tech platforms; it is far less absorbed by concentrated media power inside newspaper and broadcast markets. Indeed, the conception appears to be that, particularly in relation to news given its importance to the democratic process, legacy media need *additional* protections from digital intermediaries in the shape of new subsidies and tax breaks.[21] This ignores the fact that the online dominance of a handful of established news organizations is reproducing and intensifying existing patterns of agenda-setting power that continue to exert a substantial influence over media and political culture. Given the roles of Fox in mobilizing support for Donald Trump, of Globo in amplifying the insurgent voice of Brazilian President Bolsanaro, and the UK's tabloid newspapers in constantly urging their readers to 'BeLeave in Britain' ahead of the referendum on EU membership, it is premature to write off the impact of legacy media. As the *Sun*'s former editor, Tony Gallagher, noted immediately after the referendum result: 'So much for the waning power of print media.'[22] Traditional news outlets are leveraging their influence into the online world so that we now have 'a *shared* dominance of digital agendas by a relatively small number of institutional megaphones, be they platform monopolies, aggregators, or major conventional news organizations'.[23]

In the UK, levels of concentration of press power are actually increasing. In 2015 three companies controlled 71 per cent of national newspaper readership; by the end of 2018, the same three companies – Rupert Murdoch's News UK, DMG Media (publisher of the *Mail* titles) and Reach (publisher of the *Mirror* titles) accounted for 83 per cent of the national audience. By themselves, News UK and DMG, strong supporters of the Conservative Party and purveyors of anti-immigrant and anti-welfarist agendas, dominate over 60 per cent of the market share of national newspapers. Despite drops in circulation of their leading daily titles of approximately 25 per cent since 2015, they continue to have a prominent presence in online spaces where the *Sun* and *Daily Mail* alone account for nearly 40 per cent of total daily offline and online UK news-brand reach.[24] This also guarantees them continuing attention from politicians and, evidence suggests, from broadcasters. For example, one study of inter-media agenda-setting during the 2015 UK general election found that television news, while bound by impartiality regulations, nevertheless 'pursued a similar agenda to UK newspapers during the election campaign and followed their lead on some of the major stories'. More than half of all BBC stories on election policy issues had previously been published in newspapers, a figure that rose to nearly two-thirds of stories on Sky News, controlled at the time by Rupert Murdoch's 21st Century Fox.[25]

As previously noted, digital markets were initially conceptualized as representing the death knell of the blockbuster economy and its replacement by a 'long tail' where *niche* replaces *hit* as its overarching logic. The problem is that the evidence, at least in relation to news and information markets, does not bear out this optimism: niche products may have far more of an edge than they used to but they remain overshadowed by the size and influence of dominant sources and mainstream media. For example, after examining some 7.5 million tweets about the 2015 refugee crisis, researchers concluded that 'power, understood as visibility and ability to set the agenda through hashtags mentions and RTs, is concentrated in some accounts and hashtags that include well-established actors who already enjoy power and visibility both on and off Twitter'.[26] The power to frame the issue of migration – as with so many other issues – still remains in the hands of elite politicians, mainstream media and well-resourced lobbyists.

We can see this unequal share of voice inside the UK news landscape. While the left-wing digital native news site, *The Canary*, attracted a very creditable 817,000 UK visits in January 2019, this is less than one per cent of the traffic to the *Guardian* with nearly 104 million visits. During the 2017 UK General Election campaign period, *The Canary* outperformed the *Daily Mail* online when it came to Facebook shares of articles on the two main party leaders. Yet its actual reach was, over the same period, a tiny fraction of the *Mail*'s (one percent versus 36 percent). And in the month the election was called, page views of the *Daily Mail* website outnumbered those of *The Canary* by a factor of more than 700. Similarly, the right-wing outlet *Westmonster* saw 614,000 visits to its site in January 2019, approximately 0.6 per cent of that of the *Daily Mail* with 102 million visits. Indeed, none of the top ten news websites in the UK (measured by reach) are new start-ups; all of them are legacy newspapers or broadcasters with the BBC, *Sun*, *Mail*, *Guardian* and *Telegraph* occupying the top five positions.[27]

What does the media's concentrated power mean for journalism's analysis of pressing societal problems and for the public's right to be informed about the full range of approaches that is required to address these problems?

It means that frameworks and solutions that run counter to established positions are likely to be discredited or marginalized. Consider the impact of economics coverage that 'began from the 1980s to prioritize sources from the financial sector and business community as well as "pro-business" officials, to the detriment of voices from labour and other sections of society'.[28] It was not so much that the media 'failed' to predict the 2008 banking crisis but that, as we have already suggested, they helped celebrate the financial instruments and deregulatory landscapes that ultimately paved the way for the crisis. Coverage in the British media in the aftermath of the crisis didn't just fail to consider possible alternatives but instead repeatedly highlighted the dangers of a growing deficit with a specific focus on the need for cuts in public spending. Mike Berry, who has carried out detailed research in this area, argues that 'pro-growth policies or levying wealth, property or transaction taxes were invisible as public policy options', while the press, in particular, was crucial in 'establishing key strands of audience belief that helped justify the implementation of austerity policies'.[29]

It means that major media outlets are complicit in fostering trivial narratives about the environment that undermine the possibility of urgent debate that can lead to decisive action. All too often, news bulletins show pictures of revellers enjoying the hot weather in parks and on beaches when, in reality, the underlying story ought to be about the fact that eighteen of the nineteen warmest years on record have all been in this millennium. A study by Media Matters found that of 127 stories on network news covering the 2017 heatwave in the US, only one referred to climate change; the same organization researched TV coverage of Hurricane Harvey the same year and found that two of the main US news networks, ABC and NBC, failed to mention climate change at all in their reports.[30] When the UN's Intergovernmental Panel on Climate Change produced a report in 2019 showing how greenhouse gas emissions, deforestation and intensive farming are jeopardizing the future of agricultural land, Media Matters revealed that only seven out of twenty newspapers in the main agricultural states mentioned the report on their front page, while none of the main Sunday TV news referred to it at all.[31]

It means that where radical political alternatives are proposed, they are likely to be shot down by the mainstream media. When Jeremy Corbyn was elected as leader of the Labour Party in 2015 on a radical, anti-austerity and anti-imperialist platform, the media's reaction was immediately to go on the offensive. 60 per cent of all coverage in his first week as leader was overtly negative with only 13 per cent of stories containing positive messages. Subsequent studies of press coverage tended to confirm this initial judgement. In July 2016, researchers at the London School of Economics assessed over 800 articles in eight leading newspapers. They found that the majority of coverage was either 'critical' or overtly 'antagonistic' and argued that the press had moved from a 'watchdog' to an 'attack dog' role that was aimed at delegitimizing the Labour leader because of his willingness to challenge the political establishment. Broadcasters, expected to respect 'due impartiality', were less obviously partisan but they nevertheless happily reproduced memes about Corbyn's 'unelectability', his alleged links to terror-ists and his reluctance to send millions of people to their death by pressing the nuclear button.[32] This combination of vilification and misrepresentation was intensified in the 2019 general election and contributed to Labour's defeat and to Corbyn's resignation as Labour leader.[33]

Part of the problem is that the restricted scope of mainstream coverage is due to the media's own lack of diversity. For example, research by the Sutton Trust found that the news media is one of the most elitist sectors of British society with a substantial overrepresentation of people with a privileged educational background. While just seven per cent of the UK population is schooled privately, 44 per cent of newspaper columnists, 43 per cent of the top 100 senior journalists, editors and presenters and 29 per cent of BBC executives went to 'independent' schools; 44 per cent of columnists, 36 per cent of the 'News Media 100' and 31 per cent of BBC executives attended either Oxford or Cambridge, hardly proportionate to the less than one per cent of the UK population who studied there. The researchers identified a 'disconnect' between journalists and publics which leads to an agenda-setting that reflects the news media's own priorities and class situation and diminishes those experiences with which they are less familiar.[34]

In this situation, to what extent can public service media provide a bulwark against commercial priorities, state intervention and systematic misrecognition? In reality, there remains a stark gap between the normative vision of public service media – one that is genuinely accountable to and representative of publics and that scrutinizes elites rather than deferring to them – and the behaviour of 'actually existing' PSM organizations. Public service media are likely to be intertwined – through funding arrangements, elite capture, government diktat and unaccountable modes of governance – with the specific configurations of political power in their 'home' states. Public service media across Europe are reined in by funding crises, political attacks and, in the case of Poland and Hungary, direct political interventions including the appointment of top executives and the sacking of oppositional journalists.

Even the much-heralded independence of the BBC has been undermined. Far from retaining its autonomy from all vested interests, and delivering a critical and robust public interest journalism, the BBC has been a key institutional mechanism for reinforcing establishment 'common sense' and has represented the strategic interests of the powerful more than the disparate views of ordinary audiences. The BBC's reporting on the financial crisis was dominated by stockbrokers, investment bankers, hedge-fund managers and City analysts, while research for the Media Reform Coalition found that BBC bulletins gave nearly twice as much airtime to critics of Jeremy Corbyn than to his supporters when reporting on the internecine warfare in Labour in 2016.[35] It has reached the point where even the accomplished former World Service journalist, Owen Bennett-Jones, has condemned the

BBC's dependence on official sources and argues that 'there is plenty of evidence that the BBC, in both its international and domestic manifestations, deserves the epithet "state broadcaster"'.[36] Without significant reform, public service media are, in reality, just as likely to be embroiled in the reproduction of media power as their commercial counterparts and therefore just as likely to be part of the problem rather than the solution.

Conclusion

Media power is being consolidated at a time when continuing austerity, a climate emergency and a rising tide of authoritarianism and nationalism demand that publics be exposed to a range of perspectives and policies to address these challenges. Reproduced in the avaricious and reckless circumstances of neoliberalism, dominant media voices do precisely the opposite: they suppress alternatives and celebrate precisely the values – of private property, free markets and consumerism at all costs – that have wreaked havoc across the globe. Indeed, media power presupposes the control of resources and shared ideological commitments that allow the media to naturalize unequal social relations and to routinely celebrate a system that is fraught with tension.

Journalism is in crisis – rocked by disinformation, mocked by populist politicians and distrusted by audiences. But the threats also come from within: from traditional proprietors and 'respectable' editors and commentators, who have used their influence to uphold the status quo and to discredit new ways of organizing our public systems of communication. If we are to shrug off the oppressive relations of surveillance capitalism, data colonialism, digital dominance and widespread misinformation,[37] then it is vital that we instigate structural reform of the media, including the break-up of some of its most influential companies. To do so would be a major part of a mass campaign calling for radical social change. This manifesto is dedicated to that purpose.

2

Claiming Media Justice

Reframing media reform

Like all movements for progressive social change, the media reform movement is forced to confront the conceptual trappings of both entrenched liberalism and emergent illiberalism in mainstream media and policy discourse. This is not just a battle of ideas but a struggle over meaning. Words like 'pluralism' and 'freedom' take on acute ideological significance when applied to the media, while terms like 'fake news' or 'hate speech' have become irrevocably politicized. More than ever, against the backdrop of consensus breakdown and ever more fractured public spheres, we need new words, which capture the centrality of media reform to the politics of hope and which challenge the often technocratic, cosmetic and reductionist nature of media policy debate.

A useful starting point is the word 'reform' itself, whose progressive connotations have been hollowed out by four decades of market fundamentalism in media policy-making and wider neoliberal frameworks that categorize creeping privatization in health, education and welfare under the banner of 'reform'.[1] The notion of media *justice* comes much closer to capturing the underlying struggles of class, gender and race that are at stake when we talk about the need for more balanced, pluralistic, representative, accurate and accountable sources of news and information, or a more accessible, diverse and participatory system of cultural production. An emphasis on claiming media justice encompasses, but is not limited to, support for the individual or collective victims of press abuse. It encompasses but surpasses a rights-based approach to effecting change. Above all, it signals a recognition that piecemeal, light-touch and market-driven frameworks for regulating the media in fledgling democracies have failed. They have failed to deliver even on the modest goals axiomatic to the liberal democratic project: the protection of competition and privacy, and the pursuit of diversity and freedom.

Claiming media justice is then, at root, about seeking redress. It invokes an approach that starts *not* from a conception of emergent risks or threats to democratic media systems, but rather an acceptance that the threats have already materialized. The problem is not the future but the status quo. The greatest threat is not technology, new waves of populism or new means of foreign interference, but something much less fashionable and much more fundamental: the accumulation of agenda power in the hands of the few.

Yet it is precisely this power, as we discussed in the opening chapter, which is so often obscured, erased or misconstrued in contemporary debates about the media. This means that before we can effectively challenge the injustices of our media order, we have to confront the myths and myth-making that surround it. In particular, the progressive media manifesto must bring the ownership and *productive* power of media institutions back into the equation; it must show how and why the distributive monopoly power of platforms is not a counter-weight to the residual influence of the mainstream press, nor an actual or potential check on the spread of populism and illiberalism. On the contrary, a truly progressive media manifesto rests on an understanding of how the consolidation of mainstream media, the domination of platform monopolies and the ascendance of a new far-right politics are intimately linked and mutually constitutive.

At face value, this supposition seems at odds with the seemingly deep fault lines between the press, Silicon Valley and the politics of illiberalism. After all, when President Trump echoes and amplifies the rhetoric of the alt-right in decrying the 'fake news media' he's usually referring to CNN and never Breitbart; and when News Corp raises the alarm of 'overwhelming' market power[2] it's clear that Google has replaced even the BBC as the Murdochs' public enemy number one. Indeed, the discourse of tech monopolies, the mainstream press and right-wing populist leaders couldn't be more diametrically and ideologically opposed. And yet it is precisely the market logic of the mainstream press that has amplified and normalized the various forms of racism, xenophobia and misogyny associated with the alt-right insurgency, providing a boon for ratings.[3] And it is precisely the scale and dominance of the mainstream press at the *production* end of the media supply chain that has proved so invaluable to the intermediary business model.

In getting to the root of these underlying and largely unseen interdependencies, we can start to unpick the illusion of elite fracture and dislocation that seems so apparent in contemporary rhetorical battles around fake news, press freedom or market power. This is the most urgent task of claiming media justice in a world where much of the core lexicon of the progressive media movement has been co-opted by far-right ideologues. The injustice becomes materialized when notions of populism, racism and fake news are mobilized by the political 'centre' to delegitimize radical (left) critiques of media power, as well as progressive independent news sources.

Such accounts tend to position the mainstream press as the primary antidote to the effects of polarization, as well as the primary victim of technological disruption, often framing media policy problems in terms of saving or sustaining 'quality' news media rather than promoting and supporting independents or new entrants. This risks fostering a direction of travel that runs counter to the fundamental values of plurality and diversity in democratic media systems. Ultimately then, this chapter is an attempt to bring ownership and control back to the centre of media policy debates and the heart of the media manifesto, by cutting through some of the conceptual mist surrounding two key over-arching media policy frames: digital disruption and the disinformation order.

Rethinking digital disruption

Over the last two decades we have seen a paradigm shift in media policy thinking across the democratic world. Incumbent newspapers, broadcasters and other media producers, once the primary threats to public policy goals around plurality and diversity, are now widely seen as victims of the new media order. Conventional logic dictates that they require not so much regulatory constraint as regulatory *protection* from the predatory force of platform monopolies, and the attendant rise of competitive pressures stemming from outside the professional news realm.

This thinking rests broadly on two pillars. First, it is widely assumed that press power is becoming eclipsed by platform power as a result of the former's declining revenues and failing business models, largely considered to be the consequence of the latter's ascendance. In the early 2000s, the mass migration of advertisers from publications to platforms, combined with an emergent hyper-competitive online news environment, left publishers large and small struggling to generate income streams either from advertisers or audiences as print sales began to plummet. Around the time of the 2008 financial crisis, this yielded catastrophic predictions for the future of the news industry. Emily Bell, then head of digital content for the *Guardian*, forecast imminent 'carnage' with as many as five national newspapers in the UK going out of business by the end of the first decade of the twenty-first century.[4]

Second, a new structural dependency emerged which has left publishers almost entirely reliant for their audience reach on the referral traffic generated by the platforms, or on the terms platforms set for copyrighted content hosted on their networks. Perhaps the most vivid illustration of this dependency was the spectacular capitulation of German publishers in 2013 in their long-running battle with the platforms over ancillary copyrights. Having succeeded in lobbying lawmakers to enforce the protection of these copyrights, they lined up to offer Google royalty-free 'opt ins' after it simply excluded them from its news service.[5] Not only have platform monopolies become the primary gateways to news consumption, but they have also assumed control over the user experience, resulting in a form of editorial influence that is now said at least to rival if not overshadow that of newsrooms or news proprietors.[6]

Yet this narrative of victimhood is built in large part on conceptual flaws, evidential blind spots and unproven assumptions. For a start, market failure in journalism long predates the spread of digital media technologies and owes much to the self-destructive effects of unchecked commercialization over several decades.[7] If we take a longitudinal view of newspaper markets in much of the developed world, it is clear that the spread of digital technologies only catalysed a decline that long predated the internet and first began with the emergence of commercial television.[8]

There is also evidence to suggest that newspaper markets are to some extent stabilizing, at least at the national level. In the decade since Emily Bell's dire prediction about the state of the UK news industry, only the *Independent* ended up closing its print operations in 2013 (switching to a digital-only model) while the *Guardian* announced in 2019 it had achieved profitability thanks to its membership model, generating its highest revenues for over a decade (and mostly from digital operations).[9] Even an independent review commissioned by the UK government into a 'sustainable future for journalism' acknowledged in the same year that 'most national newspapers and regional newspaper groups are generating good profits, with margins of ten per cent or more'.[10]

Though stabilization in the newspaper industry

is unlikely to be across the board or longstanding, it is important to remember that many news outlets – and newspapers in particular – have long functioned as loss leaders for their proprietors (whether for prestige, propaganda or public interest motives). Profits at *The Times* and *Sunday Times* newspapers remain as elusive today as they did in 1981, when Rupert Murdoch convinced Margaret Thatcher that she should wave regulatory scrutiny of his intended purchase of the titles.[11]

The balance of evidence also suggests that incumbent and large-scale news brands – including newspapers – are winning the battle of referral traffic. Google News openly and explicitly favours the likes of 'CNN and the BBC' over 'local' and 'hometown' news sources.[12] while Apple News' regular digest of headlines overwhelmingly endorses established news brands over independent and alternative media.[13] And when Facebook hired a group of journalists in 2015 to monitor its trending topics algorithm, the instruction was not to pluralize sources but to boost major news stories carried by the mainstream press if they weren't trending on Facebook 'organically'.[14]

Little wonder, then, that news sources with the highest reach on Twitter are overwhelmingly established and mostly legacy news brands,[15] while

Google's news agenda 'replicates traditional industry structures more than disrupts them'.[16] Though there is some conflicting evidence in regard to the polarizing effects of intermediaries, research that examines the performance of mainstream news sources tends to suggest that their dominance is reinforced rather than challenged by these platforms.[17] In the US, recent legislation offers publishers a 'safe harbour' from antitrust law in negotiating deals with digital platforms. This threatens to shore up cartel-like collusion between dominant news content providers and intermediary monopolies.[18]

The structural disadvantage faced by smaller and independent news sources has been further exacerbated as platforms have sought to pre-empt policy interventions to tackle hate speech and fake news. Part of the problem is that algorithms are, for all their intricacy, rather blunt instruments of self-regulation that struggle to tell the difference between voicing hate speech and reporting on it.[19] But even manual interventions have caught a number of legitimate independent news sources in the net of censorship. Having controversially enlisted the help of the Atlantic Council to help combat fake news,[20] Facebook announced in 2018 the removal of more than 800 political pages and accounts, which included a number of uncontroversial independent news outlets on both the left and right of the political spectrum.[21] A year earlier, Google tweaked its algorithm in an effort to censor fake news, only to elicit an outcry from progressive independent sites, who claimed their referral traffic had dropped off a cliff edge.[22]

Notwithstanding such efforts, platforms clearly derive commercial value from relatively extremist and provocative voices, enabling figures of hate to build followers and communities on a scale unmatched in the pre-digital era.[23] But there are also commercial pressures that push in the opposite direction. With immediacy being the key driver of competition for eyeballs, major algorithms have over the last decade moved progressively from responsive to predictive functions. As a result, platforms have increasingly begun to prejudge user preferences on the balance of probabilities, favouring mainstream news brands with scale, volume and established audiences.[24] After all, in spite of declining audience trust, it is these brands that still signify issue importance – a phenomenon that researchers have coined 'gatekeeping trust'.[25] People may not agree with or believe in what the mainstream news has to say on any given issue, but they remain the primary definers of the news that *matters*.

From this perspective, it is perhaps not

surprising that the majority of those who voted for US President Donald Trump did not rely on any online platforms or news sites as their most significant source of election reporting. If anything, it was television not Twitter that handed Trump the keys to the White House. According to the Pew Research Center, television was the main news platform for 62 per cent of Republicans who supported Trump during the crucial primaries stage, compared to just 28 per cent who relied predominantly on social media or news websites.[26] Indeed, the demographics of Trump voters are broadly the inverse of active Twitter users in the US; the majority living in non-urban areas and concentrated in higher age groups,[27] in direct contrast to the majority of active Twitter users.[28]

None of this is to suggest that there exists no crisis of sustainability in some news markets – especially smaller and local markets – or an acute squeeze on newsgathering resources. But such pressures are not proxies for declining influence and waning press power and the mainstream media are not the primary victims of technological disruption. It is surely no coincidence that the script for this narrative of victimhood, invoking a co-opted and distorted vision of media justice, has been co-written by some of the world's most powerful media corporations, lamenting not just the assault on their own bottom lines, but a social malaise lurking in the shadow of tech giants. As News Corp CEO Robert Thomson remarked in 2017:

> The digital duopoly [of Facebook and Google] clearly benefited from commodifying content and rewarding sites, fake or flawed, that gamed search engines and peddled witless clickbait at the expense of provenance and professional journalism [...] That commercial and social damage has been a serious concern for many, many years, and yet other publishers have been supine in the face of this assault on principle and profit.[29]

Reconfiguring the disinformation order

Of course, the notion of victimhood in respect of digital disruption would not be sufficient on its own to convince most policy-makers of the need for regulatory intervention and protection. Any effective lobbying strategy needs to go one step further and show why the mainstream press are *too important to fail*. Here, the liberal conception of professional news norms in support of journalism's social purpose takes centre stage. It is contrasted with an apparent wild west frontier of newsgathering and distribution within 'algorithm-enabled communities'[30] where concern for such things as accuracy and balance is eschewed in the pursuit of ideological and extremist agendas.

And here too, the mainstream apostles of media (in)justice find support in much of the recent academic literature, even among media critics. In their elaboration of what they call the disinformation order, Bennett and Livingston build on a burgeoning movement to apportion much of the blame for Donald Trump's political ascendancy on alt right digital networks, amplified by right-wing partisan media.[31] Though these sources constitute the primary nodes of the disinformation order, they also draw explicit parallels with the radical left:

> There are of course some radical left networks also spreading disinformation, and engaging with fake news. Like their counterparts on the right, many on the radical left have become wary of centre parties and the corruption of democratic institutions, adding to the legitimacy crisis of modern democracy.[32]

But this exclusive location of disinformation sources on the margins of the political spectrum is at odds with the reality of news consumption during the 2016 US election. Not only were digital platforms far less used by Trump voters than television, as we have seen, but most did not even rely on Fox News – seen as the key amplifier of alt right agendas – as their main source of news.[33]

Perhaps even more surprising, some 20 per cent of Trump voters relied predominantly on one or other of the 'liberal' or 'mainstream' news brands including NBC, CBS, ABC and CNN.[34] And it turns out that Trump's brand of provocative illiberalism proved to be at least as much of a commercial boon for these networks as for the platforms. Underscoring Leslie Moonves' remark that Donald Trump was 'damn good for CBS' (as we saw in the opening chapter), a study commissioned by the *New York Times* found that mainstream media attention to Trump was more than double that afforded to Hillary Clinton and more than five times that of Ted Cruz, the second most media salient candidate in the Republican nomination race.[35] The problem was exacerbated by an overwhelming focus on personality over policy in much of the press coverage.[36]

The disinformation order also neglects entirely the wealth of accumulated evidence pointing to disinformation reverberating within mainstream news spheres. Following the conclusion of the official investigation into alleged collusion between the Trump presidential campaign and the Russian state,

Glenn Greenwald offered a searing indictment of the apparently manufactured 'Russiagate' scandal:

> [T]he contempt in which the media and political class is held by so much of the US population – undoubtedly a leading factor that led to Trump's election in the first place – will only continue to grow as a result, and deservedly so. People know they were scammed, that their politics was drowned for years by a hoax. And none of that will go away no matter how insulated media and political elites in Washington, northern Virginia, Brooklyn, and large West Coast cities keep themselves, and thus hear only in-group affirmation while blocking out all of that well-earned scorn.[37]

In the UK, the leader of the opposition has been the subject of back-to-back scandals echoing across the mainstream press, labelling him a 'terrorist sympathizer', a 'communist spy' and a 'racist'. Resembling the kind of discourse that would not look out of place in Kremlin-controlled media, broadcasters including the BBC have been implicated in repeating some of the falsehoods underpinning these labels.[38] Ironically, some of the editorial attacks were cheered on by a shadowy *counter*-disinformation outfit known as the Integrity Initiative, backed by the Foreign and Commonwealth Office and head-quartered in a disused mill in rural Scotland. When the *Sun* published an exclusive headline claiming Jeremy Corbyn was a former spy for the Soviet Union, it was not long before the single source behind the story was thoroughly discredited by intelligence experts.[39] But even after this, the notion of Corbyn being a 'useful idiot' of the Soviet regime was fermented in *The Times* by Ed Lucas,[40] a journalist directly linked to,[41] and retweeted by, the Integrity Initiative.[42]

In a further irony, many of the distortions and reporting failures in the mainstream press have been exposed and countered by the very partisan media delegitimized in the disinformation order. What's more, these radical left news sites have faced torrential attack by those that position populism and 'fake news' as an equal problem in both far-right and radical left networks. In the UK, the Canary website – a tiny news organization that employs less than a handful of journalists – found itself the target of a 'stop funding fake news' campaign in 2019. This in spite of the fact that it has signed up to the UK's only self-regulatory body officially recognized as independent and robust,[43] in contrast to all national newspapers. What's more, the Canary was the subject of 58 complaints to the regulator in 2018 – the highest of all its publishers – only two of which were upheld.[44]

This is not to suggest that radical left media are immune to the kind of distortions and falsehoods that can surface in the mainstream press, or that the latter are not capable of producing high-quality and honest journalism. Direct comparison in any case is somewhat redundant not least given the vast difference between them in scale and resources. The important point is that the mainstream media are not the antidotes to disinformation that they are often assumed to be in both academic and journalistic discourse. Nor are they the saviours of real news any more than their most ardent critics within the 'fifth estate'.

(Re)claiming media justice

The attack on radical left news sites is also – by extension and implication – an attack on radical left critiques of media power that have formed the bedrock of the progressive media reform movement for many decades and in many countries. The business of claiming media justice is therefore compelled to reclaim the legitimacy and enduring resonance of such critiques, and to reject the false equivalence with far-right populism and its often vacuous and co-opted use of terms such as fake news and media bias. It is no doubt true that amid an ever more fractured and polarized public sphere we are witnessing something of a disinformation paradigm. But it is one from which no subset of the news media ecology is immune, even if it is concentrated in the channels and networks associated with the alt or far-right.

It is surely also true that neither this phenomenon, nor its enabling algorithms, bear exclusive or even primary responsibility for the new far-right ascendancy that has gripped several democratic societies around the world. In the US at least, it seems clear that platforms, partisan media and the mainstream press all helped pave Donald Trump's path to the White House. All three amplified his message in different ways, driven by distinct commercial logics. Their respective impact was more mutually reinforcing than counter-balancing, in spite of the surface rhetoric of conflict between them. This phenomenon comes close to what scholars have termed the amplification effect or 'feedback loop', with television networks hanging on every tweet and Trump in turn responding directly to round-the-clock news feeds on both the partisan and mainstream channels.

It seems equally clear that many commercial newsrooms and platforms alike profit from the kind of outrage and incendiary rhetoric that ferments the discourse of hate; the kind that became a staple of recent election campaigns waged by the Republican Party in the US, the Fidesz Party in Hungary, the Social Liberal Party in Brazil, the Liga Nord Party in Italy and the Leave campaign in Britain's EU referendum. That is not to apportion blame but rather to acknowledge an in-built conflict between commercial drivers and ethically driven 'filters'. Neither algorithms nor mainstream newsrooms have proved reliable in checking the spread of misogynistic and racist hate speech both on and off line.

But it is professional journalists – and television news in particular – who bear special responsibility, given their unique capacity to cut across fractured audiences and information silos, alongside their long-established and much-vaunted professional news values. As Victor Pickard observed:

> Media institutions help set agendas and frame political debates each election cycle. But with Trump, they helped normalize and legitimize a candidate who never should've come close to attaining such power. Through *false equivalence* and a *lack of substantive policy coverage*, the media elevated a far-right politics that should have been delegitimized the moment it reared its head.[45]

It is also established professional news institutions that are the main perpetrators of media injustices, with a scale and impact unmatched by anything in the 'alternative' realm. In the UK, grossly distorted coverage of Muslims is not just the preserve of the tabloid press, as a recent analysis of coverage in *The Times* revealed.[46] And it was 21st Century Fox, not a 'fringe' media outlet, that was forced to settle over a $100 million worth of sexual harassment claims by women in less than a year.[47]

Conclusion

It is against this backdrop that we need constantly to unravel the myth-building behind narratives that position the mainstream media as both the victims and saviours of the new media order. We need a return to the fundamental concerns about the few who continue to exert dominance over public conversation. Above all, we need to challenge the alignment of voices and perspectives across industry, policy-making and academic communities, which conceive of the gravest threats to media justice as stemming from the fringes rather than the centre.

This is of course, in the end, an ideological force. It is the ideology of the centre that situates notions of truth, balance and moderation as the exclusive preserve of those individuals and institutions still broadly wedded to a *neoliberal* order. 'Digital disruption' and the 'disinformation order' are not valueless or neutral terms but mobilize a particular vision of media justice that legitimizes – even reifies – incumbent media at the expense of radical and disruptive new entrants. These terms absolve policy-makers of the need to tackle what remains the greatest obstacle to a more democratic media system: concentrated media power. They invoke a mythical golden age of trust and reliability when both authorities and the press exercised 'more effective gatekeeping against wild or dangerous narratives from the social fringes',[48] without asking the central questions that a truly radical and progressive media manifesto must address: effective for whom and for what ends?

3

Advancing Data Justice

As digitalization introduces new questions for media power and media justice relating to algorithms and platforms, the role of data, of the 'big' kind especially, deserves further attention. It is the generation, collection and analysis of massive amounts of data that underpins these digital developments. Celebrated for providing novel forms of insights and value creation, the turn to 'datafying' mediated content and activity has also been met with considerable concern. While the Snowden leaks first published in 2013 pointed to the intricate infrastructures that are designed to capture and analyse data about our online activities and behaviour, the subsequent scandal surrounding Facebook and Cambridge Analytica reported in 2018 shed light on the significance of an increasingly data-centric media economy for electoral democracy and public debate. The desire to quantify and tabulate social life is one that is significant in both its history and its implications. Often seen as predominantly a technical matter – the inevitable progression of technological innovation as the likes of *Wired* editor Kevin Kelly would have it – the turn to data-driven tools is as much, if not entirely, a question of politics, economics and, ultimately, social justice. As media becomes datafied and automated, we are faced with the challenge of not only maintaining the possibility of private and autonomous life, but of the very possibility for social change – deliberation, mutual recognition, trust: the actual conditions for politics.

In this chapter we will engage with the prominent focus on data as the 'currency' of contemporary media, linking it to its roots in actuarial and marketing logics that have migrated to governance at large. The kind of algorithmic 'prediction products' that have underpinned the revenue of Silicon Valley's giants and redefined the advertising industry under surveillance capitalism are fast becoming the hallmarks of contemporary decision making across social life; the same logics that determine what we see in our newsfeeds now shape our ability to get a mortgage, how we are assessed for a job, and even if we should go to prison or not. As being 'seen' through data becomes part of our everyday mediated life, what is actually at stake? While concerns about surveillance and privacy dominated much of the discussion following the Snowden leaks, and data protection regulation has come to the fore in the wake of Cambridge Analytica, a growing body of work has pointed to the need to privilege a broader politics of social justice in such discussions on data. Data justice, in this regard, concerns itself not just with individual privacy and the protection of personal data, but provides a framework that is alert to the power asymmetries inherent in datafication, the disparate impact such a development has on different social groups, the contingency of its advancement on political and economic interests, and the consequences it has for civic participation and democracy. Such a framework calls for a response that goes beyond individual self-protection, technical fixes and the ethical handling of data; and instead favours a collective response rooted in historical struggles over distribution and recognition of goods, rights and freedoms situating data in conditions of oppression and domination.

Media becomes datafied

In her extensive book on surveillance capitalism, Zuboff (2019) pivots the advent of a new form of capitalism on a particular moment in 2001 when Google started developing plans for how it might generate revenue from the creation of a global search engine.[1] Creating an infrastructure that can track user activity across the web, quantifying and tabulating such activity as data points that can be collected and analysed provided possibilities for more extensive and granular profiles of users. This, she argues, marks the beginnings of a shift from industrial and managerial capitalism to surveillance capitalism. Zuboff has advanced the notion of surveillance capitalism as a way of describing the dominant business model of the contemporary digital economy. This business model, she states, relies not on a division of labour, but a division of learning: between those who are able to learn and make decisions based on global data flows, and those who are (often unknowingly) subject to such analyses and decisions. In this model, capital moves from a concern with incorporating labour into the market as it did under previous forms of capitalism, to a concern with incorporating private experiences into the market in the form of behavioural data.

This is an accumulation logic driven by data that aims to predict and modify human behaviour as a means of producing revenue and market control.

Although the extent to which capitalism has fundamentally transformed is questionable, Google's business strategy essentially proposed a new kind of approach to advertising, one that depended on the acquisition of user data for proprietary analyses and algorithm production that could sell and target advertising through a unique auction model with ever more precision and success.[2] As such an approach became the hallmark of a rapidly growing technology industry predominantly emanating from Silicon Valley, there was a need to ensure that not only mediated communication but social life in general could take the form of data. The digital platform, Couldry and Mejias (2018: 338) argue, is the central mechanism for this transformation in that it *produces* the social for capital. That is, 'a form of "social" that makes it ready for appropriation and exploitation for value as data, when combined with other data similarly appropriated'.[3] Advancing this connected form of sociality has been instrumental in cementing a media economy privileging the dominance of Big Tech and positioning data as its central currency. The nature of social relations under surveillance capitalism is therefore extractive rather than reciprocal, bypassing dialogue and consent, and based on formal indifference to information: it is quantity rather than quality that sustains it, sourcing data from a range of infrastructures from sensors to government databases to computer-mediated economic transactions alike.[4] In recent years, a booming industry in 'empathic media'[5] has given added impetus to data-driven prediction products focused on detecting simulations of our emotions to further profile and personalize.

The personalization of media is an increasingly contentious issue that is part of a broader discussion on the value attributed to data and the assumptions made not only about the nature of technology but about the relationship between data and people and what constitutes social knowledge. Van Dijck (2014) has described it as a paradigm grounded in 'dataism', the ideological component of datafication that privileges certain forms of knowledge and social order, assuming that (objective) data flows through neutral technological channels and that there is 'a self-evident relationship between data and people, subsequently interpreting aggregated data to predict individual behavior'.[6] In other words, the drive towards datafication is rooted in a belief in the capacity of data to interpret social life, sometimes better or more objectively than pre-digital (human) interpretations. As Harcourt (2015) describes it, power comes to circulate through a new form of rationality, one that is based on algorithmically processed massive data-sets driven by a 'digital *doppelgänger* logic' in search of our data double.[7] It is such logic that informs not only the personalization of media, but the operationalism that comes with the imperative of pre-emption; a media industry increasingly organized around automated data processing and the pursuit of total information capture with the view to anticipate and respond to human actions in advance.[8]

This datafication of media has far-reaching implications, not least for democracy and governance. In providing unprecedented insights into the nature of state surveillance programmes, the Snowden leaks outlined the significance of this business model for how we are governed. The kinds of surveillance programmes revealed by Snowden are what we might think of as forms of 'big data surveillance',[9] underpinned and sustained by the corporate drive to generate and exploit user data. Programmes such as *Prism* and *Squeaky Dolphin* outlined how agencies rely on data collection from large internet companies and user engagement with mainstream digital platforms from Google to Facebook to YouTube. State governance has, in other words, become integrated into, and contingent upon, the digital economy. Moreover, it has adopted the logic of the advertising industry in its turn to algorithmically processed digital data as a way of sorting, categorizing, assessing and profiling populations with the view to inform decision-making that impacts on the lives of individuals.

The adoption of such logic goes beyond the realm of intelligence and security services that the Snowden leaks were concerned with and speaks to a broader datafication of society.[10] Eubanks (2018) has referred to a growing 'regime of data analytics'[11] in public services, while Yeung (2018) describes it as an emerging paradigm of 'new public analytics'[12] in public administration that privileges the aggregation and analysis of data to shape policy across areas of education, benefits allocation, child welfare, health and policing. While data has an extensive history in population management and has long been part of the bureaucratization of the modern state, the prevalence of approaches that rely on digital communication infrastructures, often emanating from the realm of advertising and marketing, is evidenced by the growing prominence of profiling and prediction tools in governance spaces. In this context, epistemic qualities are attributed to algorithms particularly in their ability to assess potential needs and risks, not dissimilar to the kind of credit scores generated through integrating heterogenous data sets from various sources of online and offline activity. In other words, digitally mediated data is increasingly part of shaping the contours of citizenship, determining the deserving and undeserving, the risky and the vulnerable and, ultimately, the terms upon which access to and participation in society might occur.[13]

Datafication is in this sense a 'political economic regime' in which the drive to accumulate data now propels new ways of doing business and governance. While data is not the same as profit, Sadowski (2019) argues that it shares the same logic: just as we expect corporations to be profit-driven, we should now expect organizations to be data-driven.[14] Rather than understanding data as a commodity, therefore, we can begin to see data as capital: data collection is driven by the perpetual cycle of (data) capital accumulation, which in turn drives capital to construct and rely upon a universe in which everything is made of data. Rather than breaking with financialization, datafication instead adds new sources of value and tools of accumulation. As Poon (2016) has outlined, the advent of big data has its roots in the actuarial premises of advanced capitalism and the financialization of risk.[15] This refers to a history that is also marked by the alignment of the worlds of economy and security: data infrastructures not so much melting these worlds together as much as these, in the words of Amoore (2013: 4), becoming 'elements across which the imagination of future possibilities resonates, vibrates and intensifies'.[16]

Framing what is at stake

In positioning datafication in relation to its operative logics, we can move away from the notion that this is simply a technical development, one that concerns predominantly a quantitative shift: more information shared faster. Equally, we can begin to peel away at the prevalent trend of establishing the issue within the parameters of data simply being used for 'good' or 'bad'. Neither of these engage with the turn to data-centric technologies as a distinctly political and economic development, nor do they attend to the epistemological and ontological assertions that come with understanding the social world as one that can be datafied. Rather, they advance a myth of data as a neutral technical artefact, abstract from context, upholding scientific objectivity unpolluted by human intervention and free from the convoluted space of narrative and representation, and indeed interests. As Andrejevic (2019) describes it, the imperative is to achieve 'framelessness', a medium where, with ubiquitous recording, data can speak for itself.[17] Data, on this reading, is the undeniable truth and the digital networks that fortify its accumulative logic, appear as deinstitutionalized, apolitical spaces making claims to what we naturally do collectively.[18]

Pushing back on these limited characterizations of datafication has become especially pertinent in recent years and presents itself as a primary task for researchers, practitioners and activists working in the realm of data politics. As mass data collection has come to embed itself in how media, the economy and the social are organized, the societal implications of datafication are increasingly a pressing concern. Yet making claims to what is actually at stake with such developments is itself emerging as a key site of struggle over justice. Although the Snowden leaks predominantly confirmed established arguments from several internet scholars about developments, the publication of the surveillance programmes provides a historical juncture in public debate about the nature of our digital media environments.[19] In part, it shed light on the challenges of holding the congruence of state and Silicon Valley interests to account, not least as the *Guardian* was largely vilified by the rest of the press for publishing the leaks in the first place. A concerted effort was made to present mass surveillance as an effective counter-terrorism measure, a questioning of which would jeopardize (state) security and undermine efforts to deal with social deviants. In this way, a narrative was advanced that digital surveillance is a concern only for those who have something to hide, largely justified on grounds of the limitless threats that prevail over contemporary society.

However, despite efforts to justify and rationalize the monitoring of online activity on such a massive scale, a sense of unease and worry has been a prevalent aspect of public attitudes towards digital technologies in recent years. This was only heightened when the story broke on the use of Facebook data by the political consulting firm Cambridge Analytica for the purposes of political campaigning in the run-up to the 2016 US presidential elections and the British referendum on membership of the EU. Frequent sentiments refer to a feeling of a 'lack of control' in relation to what happens to digitally mediated information about us, or an increased worry about individual privacy and our ability to freely express opinions online.[20] Yet, while such concerns are prominent among people, they are often subsumed within a sense of disempowerment and resignation to the status quo. As Draper and Turow (2019) have argued, this digital resignation is actively cultivated by technology companies who deliberately obscure, deny and bypass spaces to challenge their data collection practices.[21] Moreover, alongside allies from governments and states, Silicon Valley has mastered a discourse of inevitability surrounding big data, often couched in terms of progress and innovation, that has reached new heights in its most recent incarnation as 'Artificial Intelligence' (AI). According to this narrative, (data-driven) technology is not only naturalized as an integral part of everyday life, but is positioned as the only legitimate response to social ills, a form of 'surveillance realism'[22] or 'AI realism'[23] in which alternative imaginations for how society and technology might be organized are actively marginalized. This is key to understanding the nature and challenges of engaging with a data-fied media and possibilities for social change.

Depoliticizing datafication

It is within this context that the growing recognition of concerns about the societal implications of datafication has spurred on a host of initiatives from within both government and the technology sector itself that profess to respond to the kinds of worries that people might have about mass data collection. These have focused overwhelmingly on individual privacy and the protection of personal data as the main issues at stake. Often, we are invited to think of it as a kind of trade-off in which privacy is the price we pay for advanced efficiency and greater security that comes with technological innovation. The dominant players in Silicon Valley, perhaps none more so than Google and Facebook, have invested in elaborate advertising campaigns and public relations measures dedicated to assuring users of their privacy and the 'care' with which personal data is handled. At the level of government, the EU has been at the forefront of comprehensive data protection regulation, implementing a new General Data Protection Regulation (GDPR) Act in May 2018 said to push back fundamentally on how user data can be collected and shared. As the effectiveness of such legislation gets tested, this has been complemented by the proliferation of various initiatives across industry, government and civil society framed under the umbrella of 'ethics' that set out a number of different considerations in the development and deployment of data-centric technologies, ranging from transparency to accountability to privacy. Increasingly, this also includes the notion of 'fairness' as a way of broadening the scope beyond individual privacy, taking account of the growing focus on issues of bias and discrimination in how data is collected and processed and responding to the prominent feeling among people that they want data use to be 'fair'.[24] Academia has also been an active player in this field, often as a major beneficiary of funding from both private and public bodies to advance research on data ethics in some form.[25]

Yet, such a rapid frenzy around data ethics should also invite some caution. Big Tech has been swift in setting up its own associations, creating its own guidelines and codes to make assurances about responsible handling of technological innovation. An early offering came in the form of the Partnership on Artificial Intelligence to Benefit People and Society founded by Amazon, Google, Facebook, IBM and Microsoft in 2016, a non-profit organization created to advance best practices and public understanding. Most of these companies have also subsequently attempted to set up their own ethics boards, sometimes in partnership with academics, with varying degrees of success.[26] Governments have also joined in, establishing a number of different high-level expert groups within the EU alongside new bodies such as the UK's Centre for Data Ethics and Innovation that now finds similar counterparts in several other countries. Civil society actors, meanwhile, have congregated around data ethics as a way of pushing for more responsible uses of data in different contexts and advancing data developments 'for good', from the Open Data Institute's 'Data Ethics Canvas' to UNI Global Union's call for a 'Global Convention on Ethical AI'.

While a focus on data and AI ethics has foregrounded some prominent concerns and worries about data collection and use, it is worth reflecting on what these initiatives have meant in practice. This is especially the case as this field has flourished, in no small part down to investment from Big Tech, at the same time as Silicon Valley has overtaken the banking sector in lobbying spending and has nurtured an ever-closer relationship with political elites.[27] Although codes, guidelines and councils dedicated to data ethics in various forms have proliferated in recent years, it is not clear that these have resulted in any real intervention. Government initiatives have predominantly been set up as nominal oversight bodies without any real teeth to interfere, leaving civil society actors having to levy at the abstract level of principles and rely on the goodwill of the industry to uphold them. Corporate data ethics initiatives, meanwhile, have focused on what we might consider *micro-ethics*, an orientation around the individual practitioner, setting up a compliance regime that could be described as a box-ticking exercise that, in effect, ensures no friction with the bottom line or any engagement with fundamental questions of premise.[28]

Positioning data ethics as the primary framework within which we are to situate what is at stake with datafication therefore also risks neutralizing the kind of responses that might emerge from that. Some have described the approaches we have seen in recent years as forms of 'ethics-washing', essentially providing pathways through which the technology sector can be seen to engage with public concerns about their activities, while continuing to avoid regulation or any fundamental challenges to the dominant business model that sustains it.[29] Moreover, by actively capturing the space of data ethics, the very players who are creating, developing and directly profiting from the issues that are compounded in the datafied society, have also been the ones who have been able to dictate the terms upon which we are to understand both the nature of problems and what might be suitable responses.

In many cases, this has, unsurprisingly, meant a narrowing of focus to the data-sets or algorithms themselves, positing that the causes of harms that may emerge from data collection and use can be traced to 'insufficiencies', 'errors' or 'bias' in the design or application; causes that essentially have technological solutions, preferably through further data collection and algorithmic sophistication. We need only recall Mark Zuckerberg's almost (ironically) robotic reply, 'we're building AI for that', in response to challenges presented to him during his hearing with US Congress in 2018, to see how tech fixes have become the default retort to societal concerns within the industry.

This has been an effective strategy, one that has captured the debate on datafication far and wide. A growing community of scholars and engineers, again propped up by industry, now concerns itself with creating more inclusive data-sets, developing algorithms that can better account for diverse experiences, and – sometimes alongside the longer standing tradition of privacy-by-design, sometimes in direct contrast to it pursuing some notion of 'fairness-by-design'. We see this in the budding industry of 'bias mitigation' tools and fairness tutorials developed in spaces such as the Fairness, Accountability and Transparency (FAT*) events.[30]

Much advocacy has concerned itself with the need to have a more representative technology industry, increased ethical training for engineers, and more transparency surrounding the code behind data-driven tools. Yet, while such efforts may be very worthwhile, they also serve to divert attention away from any comprehensive *political* engagement with datafication, an engagement that might be able to contend with the power asymmetries and social stratifications emerging from this development and the interests and agendas it serves.

Towards data justice

In privileging a concern with justice, we are invited to frame the stakes of datafication in different terms, ones that situate data in relation to structural inequalities and histories of domination.[31] This is important, as it signifies an inadequacy with confining technological developments as matters of moral conscience, or ones in which challenges can be addressed through market solutions. Instead, it recognizes the need for a more systemic critique in which the parameters of debate do not begin and end with the technology itself. On this reading, the asymmetries of 'haves' and 'have nots' between different data classes are an expression of the growing concentration of power in private hands, and a shift of decision-making away from the public realm, key features of the evolving media ecology. Issues of 'bias' and discrimination in data-driven tools should not be seen as bugs in the system, but rather a structural feature; a way of socially sorting populations that align with histories of stigmatization, marginalization and exclusion. The proliferation of personalization tools and recognition software are not just a question of data protection, but are techniques that align with a genealogy of social control and suppression of dissent.

This framing of what is at stake with the datafication of media builds on some of the media justice concerns discussed in earlier parts of this book, but it also borrows from an approach to media justice that directly engages with media in terms of notions of representation and recognition in addition to distribution (drawing from Nancy Fraser), and explicitly privileges concerns of marginalized groups and issues of racial and economic justice.[32] A key aspect of this approach has been to highlight how the nature of media systems and content is intricately linked to social justice struggles, calling for different media representations and the development of alternative ownership and governance

67

structures as a way of tackling injustices. Moreover, such an understanding has called for different movements and groups, across communication rights and socio-economic rights, to unite and find common ground. While still in nascent form, the growing engagement with data justice has extended these connections, pointing to the way the burdens of datafication overwhelmingly fall on the resource-poor and the historically marginalized. This is important, as it cuts through the all-too-comfortable narrative that may in part be a consequence of the emphasis on *mass* data collection, particularly prominent in the aftermath of the Snowden leaks, which suggests that we are all equally implicated in the datafied society (a democratization of either opportunity or oppression). Rather, there is a need to recognize the way the development, advancement and impact of datafication is contingent upon deep historical social and economic inequalities, both domestically and globally.

As a starting point, this shifts the focus of what voices need to be centred in any understanding of what is at stake and challenges the current constitution of the decision-making table. It explicitly undermines the assertion that the technology industry should be able to dictate the scope of problems and solutions, let alone that engineers should be the ones to decide what constitutes 'fairness' in computational terms. Perhaps more controversially, it also challenges the idea that concerns with media and data should primarily be the domain of communication and digital rights groups. Instead, in line with Gangadharan and Niklas' (2019) notion of 'decentring' technology as a way of situating it within systemic forms of oppression, the harms that emerge from data-driven systems need to be articulated by those who are predominantly impacted and those who understand the history of such oppression.[33] That is, issues pertaining to data need to be integrated into a broader social justice agenda, one in which definitions of problems and solutions may not actually be about data.

In taking such an approach, we are invited to turn our attention to focus on what function data (its collection and analysis) serves in different contexts, the social and political organization that enables it, and who benefits. This opens up the parameters of response. Take, for example, the case of image and facial recognition technology and its growing use by both private and public actors. Initial responses to such phenomena overwhelmingly focused on the 'algorithmic injustices' that emerge from the difficulties much of this technology has in recognizing the faces of certain groups, in particular black women.[34] Google has been widely condemned for its classification of images of black female faces as animals on its image search,[35] while the trialling of facial recognition technology by police in the UK has been publicly challenged by researchers who point out the high error rates in identification, sometimes as high as 90 per cent.[36] Often, the poor workings of this technology are said to be down to skewed data-sets that lack adequate representation of minority groups, especially at the intersection of gender and race, or poor algorithmic design.

On first take, this has led to calls for ways to 'correct' recognition technologies by diversifying databases and variables. Indeed, the technology industry has welcomed inclusivity as a social justice agenda (IBM paid millions to broadcast an advertisement during the 2019 Oscars ceremony on this very theme). Yet, while approaching justice concerns through such measures and finding ways of addressing misrepresentations is important in a context where digital oligopolies hold so much power over how we come to understand the social world, it is crucial that the engagement does not end there. How people are algorithmically recognized and represented make practices of discrimination and marginalization salient; as such, the debate needs to pave a path to engage with the actual conditions of such practices of discrimination and marginalization. Making 'better' working technology does little to address those questions.

In fact, a significant movement is emerging around a more substantial engagement with data justice that approaches technology as part of a long-standing history of injustices. In some instances this is framed around an abolitionist agenda as articulated by groups such as the StopLAPDSpying Coalition and the Data for Black Lives initiative, that call for a divestment of resources into oppressive data systems as part of a resistance aimed at reinvesting in communities.[37] Here, the focus is not to make current technologies more efficient, but rather to recognize how technology has meaning and impact in relation to the inequalities manifest in capitalist exploitation and a history of state violence. The call is to ban surveillance tools such as facial recognition systems, and to 'abolish big data'[38] that is used to measure and profile people. Alongside this, initiatives within and around Big Tech have started to focus on the relationship between oppressive technology systems and the labour relations that sustain them. The Tech Workers Coalition, for example, has prioritized a focus on labour organizing as a way of advancing solidarity between software engineers and social justice movements, engaging the technology sector in walk-outs and workplace protests over exploitative practices and unjust technology. For instance, in 2018 Google employees successfully pushed back on the company's involvement with the military on Project Maven, an initiative to use AI to improve the surveillance capabilities of drones, and as part of the wider #TechWontBuildIt campaign, Amazon workers have stopped initiatives to develop facial recognition technologies with law enforcement. A growing coalition of groups has also been actively organizing around technology companies contracted by the US Immigration and Customs Enforcement unit (ICE), most notably Palantir, in an effort to position technology workers in relation to migrant solidarity. More recently, Amazon workers staged a walkout as part of the 2019 global Climate Strike in recognition of the role of Big Tech in climate change and environmental degradation.[39]

Conclusion

These efforts, while still nascent and geographically confined, privilege organizing and point to the power of solidarity as a response to the operative logics of datafication. Moreover, they centre social justice concerns in a way that does not seek to 'fix' or 'correct' data-driven tools or to focus on more ethical handling of data, but that instead forces us to question the premises of their development to begin with. The engagement is political from the outset, situating technological optimization in context, and asks us to imagine alternative ways of organizing society and the nature and role of technology within that. Much of the current work of data justice is precisely at the level of imagination, breaking through the stifling parameters of what is considered acceptable conflict, and pushing back against dominant logics of data accumulation. A big part of this needs to be oriented towards solidarity building and for social justice movements and impacted communities to have a bigger role in articulating both the nature of challenges and possible solutions. This also speaks to a need to connect questions of the governance, ownership and uses of data to wider debates on economic democratization and civic participation. The fight for a just media ecology, now datafied and entrenched in an ever-more powerful technology sector, is part of a broader vision of alternative ways of organizing public goods, political process and cultural expression that pushes back on the centralization of control and that facilitates local and citizen-centred decision-making. As such, establishing and enforcing data rights such as the ones expressed in the GDPR is only one part of the puzzle. An engagement with data justice must situate this in relation to more fundamental questions about the premise of a datafied media, questions that highlight the urgent need for radical alternatives to a datafied status quo that privilege deliberation over pre-emption, recognition over identification, and equality over optimization.

4

Articulating a Politics of Hope

As set out in Chapter 1, our media manifesto embraces a politics of social change. It proclaims that above all else, and despite the dire social and political circumstances we find ourselves in, change *is* possible. As Chapter 1 also argues, change cannot be fathomed without a concept of power. For critical media scholars interested in understanding what is wrong with the media (and society) and how they could be fairer and more equal, our subject of analysis is not the media per se but media power. While political struggles over the reproduction of everyday social relations are shaped by technologies and systems of communication, they are not subsumed by them. Political imaginaries are relational in complex ways. They are bound up in the matrices of lived existence that are social as well as structural, that determine what is, what fails, and what might be. In other words, media power is not unidirectional, totalizing or fixed because it only exists in relation to other forms of power, not least that of people power.

'The people' are conceived in various ways in the field of media and communications: as consumers/users of media content (the audience), as producers of media content, as public citizens, as protestors/activists, and most recently as prod-users (describing the ability of the audience to consume, produce and disseminate content in the digital age). We used to talk about media power and audience power in distinction. The one disproved the other. Media exerted power through ideological dominance closely tied to other forms of structural power, including the state and capital. Put crudely, the media were seen as part of a capitalist class that sought further profit and capital accumulation, and that promoted the dominant ideology of ruling elites, creating new levels of social stratification that engendered new and persistent forms of domination. Then the field began increasingly to acknowledge that audiences are not simply cultural dupes but rather engage actively with the processes of meaning making and are variously able to resist dominant media narratives, manipulate imagery and information for their own ends and create oppositional meanings, revealing social and political agency. And, of course, we also use the media to mobilize political protest, make our own media content and organize for political change.

But while these debates may have moved on (largely in response to changes in technology), the same questions about who holds the balance of power pertain. Just as the active audience was deemed able to resist symbols and narratives drenched in hetero-patriarchy, they never seemed likely to be able to overturn it. Indeed, hetero-patriarchy is still very much with us and some would say is advancing in aggressive ways.[1] Similarly, the activist audience is able to use social media to mobilize social protest but seems unlikely to be able to overthrow global capitalism. And, while alternative media producers can circulate oppositional and counter-hegemonic content with increasing ease, legacy media still dominates the media landscape.[2] Even when digital activism was sometimes (and wrongly) credited with sole responsibility for the uprisings that came to be known as the Arab Spring, more measured analyses have noted how elite power often works behind our backs and out of view and is largely unaffected by major forms of protest such as Occupy, the Black Lives Matter or #MeToo movements. At best, these movements have brought to the fore a politics of recognition that has forced the enduring inequalities and oppressions of class, race and gender into view (no small feat). But at worst these movements offer up an illusion of democracy – 'look how liberal our societies are to allow and engage with such large-scale political remonstrations'. As political protest grows around the world from pro-democracy protests in Hong Kong to climate change strikes in many nations, so we also have to recognize that global inequalities between the rich and the poor, the powerful and the powerless are increasing, while environmental degradation continues apace.

So far, so unhopeful. But what this tells us is that the media may not be the best place from which to start. To understand both forms of power *and* the likelihood for progressive social change requires a deeply contextual analysis that can take account of social, political, economic, cultural, technological and environmental dynamics. Our media systems are indelibly connected to the political and economic systems of which they are a part. In the majority of countries across the globe, this system can be described to a lesser or greater extent as global capitalism. The brutal form of capitalism that dominates now has massively increased inequality with the accumulation of wealth in ever fewer hands;[3] has led to increasingly precarious and insecure labour;[4] with increases in poverty;[5] massive environmental degradation as a result of extractive relations to nature;[6] alongside the hollowing out of democracy by market forces[7] and the corporate capture of political parties at the transnational level by global finance.[8] These contemporary characteristics of advanced capitalism form the social, political and economic relations within which our media systems exist; they shape everything from who owns what, to the forms of labour, the nature of production, the means of exchange, the operation of the markets and the various stresses and injuries these exert on daily lives lived in debt, insecurity and fear.

Yet it is from these ashes that we can find the sparks of hope. When the financial crash happened in 2008, capitalism was shaken. People dared to venture that capitalism was not the only show in town, even if they were at a loss about what to replace it with. Over a decade on and people's faith in the system has plummeted. It is now common parlance that there is also a crisis of trust in the institutions of the state and particularly in the government, with 67 per cent of people saying that the government do not deliver on policy promises that protect average people.[9] Governments have lost sight of their obligation to act on behalf of citizens and have allowed themselves to become subservient to economic forces[10] leaving few people feeling that they have a part to play in this thing called democracy.[11] Politics has become something that is done to people and places not by people in places. Political parties, with a few important exceptions, have become captured by elites and are seen as increasingly irrelevant by the public. Politicians don't carry out manifesto pledges and exist in a deeply entangled relationship with mainstream media that is strangling the democratic purposes of both.

Representative liberal democracy has been eviscerated and the media, as we have argued in the previous chapters, are part of the problem. In a political economic system that has massively increased inequality and poverty through the reduction of social welfare to the poor and by an increase in financial advantage to the rich (for example, through cutting corporation tax), it should come as no surprise that we have a media system where concentration of ownership is increasing and demonization of the poor, the working class, black people, Muslim people, trans people, is commonplace. Neoliberal governments have no interest in fundamental economic reform because their primary constituency is the wealthy elite (who fund their campaigns and vote for them ensuring the continued success of their businesses and accumulation of wealth).

But with living standards collapsing, the climate in crisis and young people ever more aware that they are unlikely to have the same quality of life as their parents, many people are beginning to rebel against an economic system hell bent on profit at the expense of their futures. Events such as the collapse of the main parties in the French presidential elections of 2017, the election of Donald Trump and the decision taken by UK voters in 2016 to leave the European Union, have brought to the fore the economic dislocation that has taken place since the 1980s revealing deep class, generational and ethnic divisions. Marginalized voices have kicked back against a post-war party system that has failed them and a professional political elite that has largely ignored them. An important element of this elite is made up of the media.

The rest of this chapter explores where we might go to for resources of hope, with a specific focus on how the media might play a progressive role. It considers examples in civil society where different relationships of mutuality and democracy are emerging and how media are (or could be) part of a solution: co-operative forms of media ownership, collaborative partnerships between public and private sectors; alliances of workers and communities seeking to meet local news needs and to create new more democratic forms of mediated existence. What can we learn from these endeavours and how might the media be reconccived through a politics that attempts to rebalance power and wealth away from the few to the many and protect and regenerate the planet?

Considering the alternatives

Over the last decade a whole raft of political alternatives to a neoliberal politics and practices has emerged that attempts to respond to some of the worst vagaries of capitalism. Not all of these alternatives extend beyond capitalism and are able to offer a transformative politics based on a different type of social order. Some stand accused of working within and accommodating capitalism – making it more humane, perhaps, but never transcending the basic premise that society is structured by the accumulation of capital that will forge class privilege and power. The reformist agenda of a liberal democratic response falls into this camp. It wants to strike a compromise with capital and shore up the welfare state but rarely creates the conditions for taking capital away from capital.

One example relating to the media is the attempt to regulate commercial press in the UK and to introduce a fair, effective and independent system of regulation based on the recommendations that emerged from the Leveson Inquiry.[12] This was an attempt at managing the worst practices of commercial journalism and to limit the damage to members of the public and to democracy. It failed because the mainstream media simply refused to comply and the consequences for non-compliance that were built into the regulatory framework were neutralized.[13] It also failed because politicians ran scared of the power of the mainstream commercial press to scupper their election chances through adverse media coverage.[14] When large media corporations dominate a media market, this power cannot be underestimated. A liberal reformist agenda simply focused on consumer regulation (i.e. the ability to make more effective complaints) will never change a market-driven media and communications system charged (and some would say overwhelmed) by commercialism.

The same debate applies to the control of big data in the digital age. Is this about giving individual citizens more control over their own data, including the granting of individual property rights to personal data or implementing means of informing and consenting data subjects such as the European Union General Data Protection Regulation (GDPR)? Or is it rather about collective ownership and control through the creation of digital data and information commons in the hope that the power dynamics between data givers and data profiteers will be equalized?[15] Ultimately, any approach to reform that focuses on regulating corporations (media and technology companies included) to promote social, democratic and environmental objectives assumes that environmental degradation, rising monopoly power and increasing inequality are not a consequence of a capitalist political economy and can simply be fixed through a bit of state intervention around the edges and judicious tweaking of regulation by enlightened governments. Yet these are the very same governments that have failed so dismally in these regards over the last few decades.

Modern capitalism resides on the complex relationship between the neoliberal market and the neoliberal state. To address meaningfully the consequences of climate change, massively reduce inequality and eradicate poverty, would destabilize the power relations that underpin finance-led growth. For example, if the mainstream press industries do not attempt to maximize their profits in any way they can today, they will probably not exist tomorrow. This is particularly true when their main competitors are now global tech industries with far more capital and power than the press industry could ever have imagined. In these fiercely combative commercial circumstances, anything is up for grabs in the pursuit of profit and the public interest or democratic intent appear as no more than quaint values of a time gone by. Cut-and-paste journalism is the norm, sponsored content and advertorials begin to replace news, and clientelism is welcomed. Media corporations will undermine regulation, lobby governments for special treatment (often using the rhetoric of press freedom to disguise corporate libertarianism), sack journalists, reduce wages and wilfully sideline any notion of environmental responsibility.

Genuine alternatives need to be located in newly imagined political strategies. The combined elements of democracy and ownership are key. The UK Labour Party has proposed a series of policies aimed at democratizing ownership of the British economy.[16] These range from nationalization, to worker ownership funds, to boosting support for the co-operative sector. They are useful starting points, with some significant repercussions for the media and tech sectors. But if we are to reimagine our media futures, this will require not just alternative policies but also an alternative politics. Such a critique begins from a concern with the problems with which a capitalist economy has left us: burgeoning inequality and poverty, global warming, the biospheric damage from a dominant economic system powered by fossil fuels and predicated on endless consumption and growth that concentrates economic and political power in the hands of oligarchs and autocrats. To change this direction of travel requires political and economic alternatives to this system that are just and inclusive, ecologically wise and socially regenerative shifting economic and political power back to communities and democratic institutions.

Conceiving of a media that supports a newly imagined democratic economy means conceiving of a world post-capitalism. It means breaking away from a capitalist economy to something that looks more like a citizen's economy or a solidarity economy. Taking account of the key elements of democracy and ownership, what might this look like? We can point to three key normative criteria that are required if we are to begin to articulate a politics of hope and apply it to the media.[17] To be transformational all three criteria must be met.

Articulating a Politics of Hope

1. Wholesale egalitarianism

Egalitarianism refers both to external structural factors relating to the broader environment that media organizations function within and to internal structural factors relating to the workforce and working practices of the organizations themselves. The principle of egalitarianism clearly runs counter to the concentration of media ownership endemic across the globe with the tech giants now the largest oligopolies the world has ever seen. Mergers, takeovers and consolidations of media industries accumulate great wealth and great power in ever fewer hands. Limiting concentration of media ownership is vital but only takes us so far. It may relax the stranglehold of power that certain media corporations exert but it does not necessarily alter the neoliberal nature of the system they operate within. So it is also crucial to enable, support and sustain forms of media ownership that are not for profit and fully independent of commercial pressures and government preferences, are organized co-operatively and democratically and are responsive to the needs of the communities that they serve rather than at the behest of the market. The principle here is for new models of ownership, fully responsive and accountable to the needs of the communities they serve, that redistribute and circulate wealth rather than extract it.

In a context in which mainstream media industries are largely bastions of privilege for political and economic elites and operate with fierce hierarchies resistant to change, publicly owned organizations may appear to be a viable solution. For example, public service media such as the BBC are often seen as the best redress for a contemporary journalism marked by hyperpartisanship and hypercommercialism with the ability to offer journalism independently of the state or market, inclusive of diverse voices and with space for more critical coverage. But, as Freedman (2018: 206) argues, the BBC 'is a compromised version of a potentially noble ideal: far too implicated in and attached to existing elite networks of power to be able to offer an effective challenge to them'.[18] As noted in Chapter 1, despite its claims to be impartial and independent, the BBC has always sided with the elite and been in thrall to those in power. Over the last three decades, the BBC's independence has been steadily eroded and its programme-making increasingly commercialized.

Broadcasting in the UK was originally regulated according to public service principles. That model has been increasingly marginalized as the BBC has become more and more subject to a market-based regulation. Currently, BBC activities have to be balanced with consideration for competition through 'public value' tests. They are also subjected to 'market impact assessments' by Ofcom, the UK's communications regulator, which has been criticized for privileging consumer interests over those of citizens. Severe funding cuts, particularly in recent years, have also caused the BBC's editorial culture to become more conservative and risk-averse. Mills (2018) and the Media Reform Coalition (2019) argue that adequate, secure public funding that is independent of governmental control is the pathway to real political independence and insulation from the market-based approach that has eroded the BBC's public service ethos.[19] Rather than returning to the top-down, statist model on which the BBC was founded, to fulfil its public service promise the BBC must become a modern, democratized public platform and network, fully representative of its audiences and completely independent.

Another relevant model of democratic ownership is the co-operative: an autonomous association of people who have come together voluntarily to meet their common economic, social and cultural needs and aspirations through a jointly owned and democratically controlled enterprise. Co-operatives are based on values of self-responsibility, democracy, equality, equity and solidarity. As such, they eschew gender, social, racial, political or religious discrimination and pursue equity through things like education and training. Co-operatives work for sustainable community development through policies approved by members. They are concerned with the nurturing of people and communities and democratic self-rule. It has been argued that co-operative ownership increases employment stability and increases productivity levels by discouraging an approach based on short-termism for shareholder return and the use of low-wage labour.[20] As co-operatives are collectively owned and controlled, they are also more democratic and responsive to internal demands for more egalitarian employment and working practices. There is no employer and employee but a membership of worker-owners who are no longer solely answerable to capital; rather, capital serves the co-operative that is democratically organized and governed.

Egalitarianism means getting rid of inequalities and so is also related to the internal plurality of media organizations. An egalitarian media will recognize ways in which media have held certain people back – black people, old people, disabled people, working-class people – and will seek to counter those forms of discrimination by taking special measures to compensate for the social and economic inequalities of unjust social structures in full recognition of the different yet connected structural conditions of class, racial and hetero-patriarchal domination. The majority of mainstream media organizations are alarmingly lacking in diversity in output and in the workforce. Egalitarianism would require a major power shift in the general media landscape away from capital-hungry commercial media organizations and also in how power is shared within media organizations themselves. A shift that recognizes egalitarianism is not just an economic concern but also a social and political one too.

2. *Substantively meaningful democracy*

Just as a strong egalitarianism in the media goes beyond plurality of media ownership, so a substantively meaningful democracy goes beyond liberal versions of democracy, with their emphasis on individual rights and jurisprudence, to reconnect with a democratic tradition premised on equality, participation and popular sovereignty. In practice, this will also involve a strong sense of localism and community managed resources (including local media) run sustainably with mechanisms to progress equality and to prevent anyone taking unfair advantage. This fits most comfortably with the notion of 'subversive commoning' proposed by Birkinbine (2018). If we see the media as part of a shared public information and communications resource necessary for a healthy functioning democracy – a form of public utility – then we have to shift from viewing them as primarily competitive corporate entities to shared resources that can be co-owned and/or co-governed by the users and media workers according to their own rules and norms[21] as part of the commons. This relates to physical spaces that are shared or pooled;[22] the co-production of the resource; the means of maintaining that resource; as well as the mode of governance – how decisions are made collaboratively through collective problem-solving to distribute and use the resource.

Co-operatives, as discussed above, are democratic organizations controlled by members who jointly participate in setting policies and making decisions. Media co-ops are on the rise. The Global Newsletter for Co-operatives active in Industry Services (CICOPA) reported that in 2017 there had been a 27 per cent increase in co-ops in the field of information and communications around the world with many emerging in response to the need to preserve pluralism, escape commercial and state pressures and ensure independent journalism. Most of these are worker co-operatives with democratic governance at their core and the majority operate in Europe.[23] Many face issues of lack of finance, regulatory complexity, tax and administrative burdens but, nonetheless, are increasing in number. Part of the growth is due to the emergence of platform co-operatives where users and/or workers ultimately own and control the platforms based on principles of economic fairness, training and democratic participation in the running of online businesses.[24]

Worker co-ops are owned and run by the people who work in them, who have an equal say in what the organization does, how it develops and an equitable share of the wealth created. In Cairo the online news site *Mada* was born out of the crisis in 2013 and formed by a group of journalists who had lost their jobs and were worried about the future for independent journalism in Egypt. They describe their journalism as the kind that constantly challenges, raises questions and proposes different possibilities. They operate an open and ongoing editorial conversation on the ethics of their journalism especially with regard to protecting the rights of the oppressed and the vulnerable and preserving the privacy of sources. The workers run the business themselves, co-operatively. In the US, the Banyan project is attempting to respond to the demise of local newspapers by helping to seed independent community news co-operatives that would be professional and trustworthy. Although no news co-ops have yet launched, the objective is to nurture sustainability and to empower civic engagement and community involvement. It promotes a consumer co-operative model with reader-members electing the boards of local news co-ops and paying an annual membership fee. The Banyan project aims to provide the tools and digital publishing platform needed with the intention of increasing community events and strengthening civic infrastructure.

In the UK, *The Bristol Cable* is changing the face of local journalism as a grassroots community-led media co-operative. It prints a free quarterly magazine with a circulation of 30,000 copies and publishes investigative and community-led journalism regularly online. It also delivers free media training, equipping local people with the skills to report on issues that are important to them. It is funded by over 2,000 members, each paying a small monthly fee (who all have a say and own an equal share in the co-op), by foundation support and crowd funding. Income is also generated from advertising in the print edition regulated by an ethical advertising charter determined by members.

Each year, its members vote on the annual budget, the overall focus for content and who sits on the board of directors. They insist on democratic decision-making throughout the organization. Media co-ops like *The Bristol Cable* are trying to figure out what workplace democracy could be in the media industry – from who gets to do what jobs, to who makes decisions on content and resource distribution.

3. Financial and environmental sustainability

Media institutions across the globe are facing multiple crises: of funding, trust, representation, accountability and legitimacy. In many of the countries that make up capitalism's core, the newspaper and magazine industry is in serious decline as large digital intermediaries gobble up the majority of advertising revenue. Much of the debate about the sustainability of the news industry circulates around debates relating to this 'broken business model'. Local news, in particular, is increasingly under threat. In the UK, the majority of the population (57.9 per cent), is no longer served by a local daily newspaper.[25] To retain high levels of profitability, media corporations have closed or merged titles and cut jobs, often moving journalists long distances away from the communities they serve and no longer providing content of relevance to them. In short, a profit-driven response means they become ever more unsustainable.

However, if we shift our perspective from one of media as a source of profit to media as a resource for the public good, then the question of financial sustainability becomes a rather different one: a means to pay journalists a decent living wage in good working conditions to deliver journalism in the public interest rather than maximize shareholder profitability. *The Bristol Cable* most closely fits the description of a multi-stakeholder co-operative (MSC) whose membership includes both the workers and readers. MSCs offer a means of financial sustainability through membership payments. *The New Internationalist*, a magazine on human rights, politics and social justice, describes itself as one of the largest media co-operatives in the world. Founded in 1973, it became a workers' co-op in 1992 and then an MSC in 2017. By 2019 it had over 3,600 investor members who have a say in how the magazine develops. Becoming an MSC has given it long-term financial sustainability and enabled it to do more investigative and long-form journalism. *The Ferret*, based in Scotland, is also a co-operative run by its members and funded by subscriptions, donations, paid for stories or material and grants and gains its following from being democratic and having a clear public purpose.

Treating news media as a necessary part of a communication commons has also led lawmakers in the US state of New Jersey to establish a 'civic information consortium' in which journalists would collaborate with public universities to report on local issues and have set aside $5 million to support the initiative.[26] Elsewhere, direct press subsidies are used either to maintain struggling news organizations in order to preserve media diversity and pluralism (e.g. in Canada, France, Denmark Netherlands, Norway) through such things as state aid for distribution or export, support for the internal training of journalists, or to support newspapers in minority languages (Finland). In the UK, the Media Reform Coalition has suggested that local papers should be treated as community assets and, whenever a paper is up for closure, irrespective of (perceived) profitability, it should first be offered to local journalists themselves with alternative models of media ownership (such as local co-operatives) so as to remove the emphasis on large profit margins.

Infrastructural support for media plurality needs to go further than simply recognizing the necessity of guaranteeing citizens' access to a wide range of diverse information and debate for a flourishing democracy. To be fully sustainable we need to put citizens at the centre of democratic media governance too. An approach based on the commons is aimed at strengthening the collective solidarity of workers and offering mutual life support to all inhabitants. A media *commons* is by definition sustainable.

Conclusion

What we are witnessing through a range of approaches – loosely based on the commons, including non-market ownership structures such as media co-operatives, and other forms of radical intervention into media markets – is the re-establishment of the value of the public, of the public good and of public goods outside the public/private dichotomy for a more equal, more democratic and more sustainable society. A new politics (applicable to the media) must dismantle inequalities and the day-to-day oppressions and injustices on which the current neoliberal order depends; it must develop different ways of doing substantively meaningful democracy; and build economic power that is owned and governed by those whose lives it affects. Finally, it must re-appropriate the spaces we inhabit for the social good of all and, in particular, for those who are currently exploited and excluded.

If this seems fanciful, then we would do well to learn from Wright (2010), who suggested that we are best off conceptualizing alternatives to the status quo on the basis of the anti-capitalist potential of things that actually exist. He called these 'real utopias' because not only do they exist in practice but they reveal actual emancipatory possibilities.[27] They are far from perfect – in particular, it is often hard to see how they can shift issues at the macro level such as global finance, global warming, global inequalities and global justice – but in them we can find resources for hope, spaces for action and prospects for non-capitalist emancipatory media futures.

5

Conclusion: A Manifesto for Media Reform

As Erik Olin Wright has argued, the task of emancipatory social science is to pave a path to viable alternatives through first elaborating a systematic diagnosis and critique of the world as it exists. We need to understand the motivations of media organizations and the dynamics of datafication in order to question their legitimacy; and we need to recognize media policy and regulatory issues in terms of what Hancher and Moran called 'ideological constructions'.[1] We need to ask about the functions that various institutions perform in the new media political economy, as well as the interests served by data collection and analysis in any given context. These are not questions that can be answered by taking technology – or the conventional narratives of digital disruption – for granted. They require us to look beyond the means of communication alone as the entry-point, or by focusing solely on data or journalistic ethics. These questions demand that our diagnosis is political. To challenge media power and to secure both media and data justice requires political engagement: with media organizations, policy-makers, activists and civil society; with the processes and purposes of datafication as part of the DNA of contemporary capitalism; and with the discursive frameworks that define the scope and limits of change.

The previous chapters have attempted to embody precisely this spirit. This manifesto for media reform builds on extensive academic research into the multiple ways in which our media and communications systems fall short of providing citizens with accurate, diverse and representative media that is capable of informing and nourishing the kind of inclusive public debate that is the lifeblood of functioning democracies. But a manifesto is also concerned with social change. In its political endeavour to develop socialist strategies for radical media reform, the manifesto suggests some key principles on which change should be premised: wholesale egalitarianism, meaningful democracy and financial and environmental sustainability that situates the manifesto in a broader, visionary and emancipatory politics for social, political and economic transformation.

Conclusion

This concluding chapter builds on the arguments developed in the preceding chapters by pulling together a raft of potential strategies and policy proposals for media reform that are both practical and radical.[2] In some places these have already experienced a degree of success; in others they remain contested. While we recognize the importance of local and regional contexts and specificities that we don't have the space to deal with here, we believe that the proposals can still offer a key resource of ideas for media change. What follows are generic proposals that we think offer different ways of advancing struggles for media democracy and data justice.

The chapter encompasses four parts. First, we set out a series of recommendations aimed at forging a new 'future proof' framework for media plurality. Second, we summarize key proposals for a more democratic, diverse and devolved public service broadcasting. Third, we elaborate the urgent steps any government must take in order to restore faith in a free, accountable and sustainable press. Finally, we map out reform measures in the broader arena of digital media policy and the need for developing innovative tools and solutions to emergent problems.

A Manifesto for Media Reform

A framework for media plurality

In the majority of countries around the world, the trend is for media ownership at both local and national level to be more concentrated in ever fewer hands, raising increasing concerns about concentration of media power exerting undue influence over politicians, impacting on diversity of media content, promoting clientelism and creating an ever more impoverished public sphere. In the UK, the latest evidence shows that just three companies dominate 83 per cent of the national newspaper market (up from 71 per cent in 2015). Even when online readers are included, just five companies account for more than 80 per cent of the combined markets. The print circulation of newspapers may be shrinking, but the prevailing evidence suggests that the audience reach of the largest titles – including the *Sun*, *Daily Mail* and the *Guardian* – is increasing. What's more, recent studies have shown the enduring influence that national newspapers have over the wider news agenda, including television news and the BBC.

Around the world, mergers and acquisitions of media companies continue to condense media power with little control or intervention. And let us not forget the digital giants that constitute the largest concentrations of power that the world has ever seen. As these forms of media concentration increase, it becomes ever harder for new and innovative initiatives to emerge and survive. This is especially vital in the area of news and current affairs that plays such an important role in shaping decision-making, political participation and activism. To counter increasing concentration of ownership and to promote meaningful plurality – i.e. not simply more voices saying the same thing but a system that expresses a range of conflicting voices and perspectives – we suggest that governments must, as a bare minimum:

- Establish a plurality measurement framework that can address the complexities in assessing cross-market audience share in radio, TV, print and online news markets, drawing on a mix of methodologies and taking into account not just quantitative measures of reach and consumption, but also qualitative data on impact, especially in respect of the wider media agenda.
- From the above determine a set of thresholds based on cross-market audience share that will ensure plurality of ownership and, where necessary, redress existing concentrations. These thresholds should be subject to regular periodic

assessment by an independent regulator. Where thresholds are exceeded, this should trigger intervention and remedies aimed at promoting not just plurality in terms of numbers, but a rich ecology of media at both the local and national level, including commercial, public service and independent not-for-profit vehicles.

- Digital intermediaries should not be included in the cross-market measure, since that assumes all news consumption via intermediaries is inherently pluralistic. Instead, they should be subject to bespoke monitoring for plurality. Both the metrics and performance of the news algorithms of intermediaries should be scrutinized and monitored by an independent regulator to ensure that they do not unduly favour particular types of news providers and voices over others, at both the individual and aggregate levels.

- Digital giants should contribute financially to maintaining a public interest news ecology through hypothecated taxation. One way of doing this would be through a levy imposed on the country-specific revenues of companies with more than a 20 per cent share of online search or social networking markets.[3] The money could be redirected to an independent public funding body and targeted at those vehicles and forms of public interest journalism that have become increasingly squeezed in the digital news environment. To ensure that new money does not simply rescue failing legacy providers or reinforce concentration of ownership but rather extends and enriches media plurality, this money would need to be directed towards new models of not-for-profit, public interest journalism.

- Alternative models of media ownership – such as co-operatives and employee buyouts – that promote equality and financial security over shareholder returns should be encouraged. These ownership models are a response to the need to broaden the range of voices involved in decision-making, which in turn aims to ensure that our media meet a wider range of needs and serve a more diverse set of interests.[4] This can only be realized through ownership models that embody genuine agency and collectivism. This could be achieved through improving access to finance, support for charitable status and measures like tax relief or direct subsidies (as above) that are designed to sustain a plurality of outlets without compromising independence.[5]

- When news organizations close down (or merge) due to perceived lack of profitability, they should first be offered to the journalists themselves to run under alternative models of media ownership that will remove the emphasis on maintaining large profit margins.

A more democratic diverse and devolved public service broadcasting

Research shows that where independent and viable public service broadcasting (PSB) exists, citizens are better informed about public issues. But the independence and viability of PSB needs to be constantly renewed if it is to positively shape a broader media ecology in the digital age. The BBC is often held up as the model of public service broadcasting, yet over the last three decades its independence has been steadily eroded and its programme-making increasingly commercialized. In recent years in particular, its funding has been severely cut and its editorial culture has become increasingly conservative. Public service content needs to be delivered through modern, democratized public platforms and networks and to operate autonomously of government and the market. In particular:

- Governing bodies of all public service providers (i.e. both existing PSBs and any future public models) should be elected by citizens and include staff representation.

- An independent non-market regulator should oversee the constitution of the organizations involved, standards of democratic governance and programme-making, the sustainability of the funding and ensure it is acting solely in the public interest.

- Programme-making and editorial functions should be decentralized and devolved to regions with a system of localized, democratic management, and commissioning established to better respond to more local needs, create better relationships between producers and citizens with more sensitivity to local social concerns and community wealth building. Regional boards should be elected by staff and citizens in the same manner as the national board and run democratically.

- Staff should be unionized and representative of the population. Ensuring adequate diversity will require complete transparency about the makeup of the workforce. This will mean publishing rigorously collected equality monitoring data at the programme and production level for all producers of content, whether in-house or external. This should include data on social class, as well as age, gender, sexuality, ethnicity, religion, disabilities and other characteristics. Delivering on diversity will also mean addressing the casualization of the workforce as precarious working conditions narrow the range of people able to produce programmes, disproportionately impacting on those from lower-income families, women, minority groups and those with disabilities.

A free accountable and sustainable press

There are serious threats to press freedom around the world, stemming from the security state and inadequate legal protections for journalists. Protecting press freedom, however, does not mean that journalists themselves are above the law or beyond accountability. Freedom of the press must go hand-in-hand with freedom of the public to assess and challenge the nature of that communication: freedom shared, not power abused. Until journalism is able to hold its own institutions of power to account, to expose its own malpractices and to challenge some of the most obvious abuses of media power, distrust in news journalism is likely to grow. Often press abuse becomes more prolific when financial imperatives loom large. So, creating a sustainable system of funding for news in the public interest is vital. Such funding should be directed at those organizations that will also extend plurality, be not-for-profit, democratically organized and function solely in the public interest.

- All news publishers must be subject to effective regulatory mechanisms that are entirely independent of the industry and of government influence and able to uphold standards, process complaints, investigate gross misconduct and promote journalism of integrity.
- News publishers should be unionized, operate a whistleblowing policy and a journalists' conscience clause that enables journalists to speak out against unethical behaviour without fear of losing their jobs.
- Independent non-profit news providers – especially at the local level – can make a unique and important contribution to democratic citizenship yet often struggle to survive in a hyper competitive digital news environment. Public funding is needed to support the growth of a wider range of civic-minded news publishers. This could be provided from a levy on the largest tech companies (suggested above) and

delivered via a range of mechanisms to preserve independence of the recipient of funds from awarding authorities. One way of doing this is via a voucher system,[6] in which every adult is given a set amount of money to spend on both national and local news outlets that meet an agreed series of criteria, such as democratic governance structures that guarantee journalist autonomy and membership of an independent and effective regulator.

- A statutory right of reply can also help to retain press standards and should be applied to all news publishers.
- Privacy protections for journalists should be in place. Journalists should be informed if and when they are placed under surveillance, since this could compromise their ability to protect sources, and to investigate and report on sensitive topics in the public interest.

Digital media policy

The preceding recommendations have focused on news provision but they are intimately connected to other areas of regulation in the digital media environment. The dominance of platform monopolies, the weakening of 'net neutrality', and the relative opacity of online political advertising all have a direct bearing on the media's capacity to support freedom of expression and inclusive public debate. We need innovative solutions to these problems, with a view to safeguarding both media freedom and access to diverse and credible sources of information online.

In his Alternative McTaggart lecture in 2018, Jeremy Corbyn (the leader of the UK Labour Party) called for a new British Digital Corporation alongside the BBC 'to rival Netflix and Amazon, but also to harness data for the public good'. The 2019 Labour Party Manifesto pledged to nationalize broadband infrastructure and provide everyone with free high-speed internet service. Clearly, the emergence of platform monopolies in search, social media and excessive content provision decimates the public value of the internet commons and exacerbates digital divides in access to diverse and credible sources of news and information. To counter this, we need to address the following:

• Giant global technology firms dominate our digital lives, extracting our data for profit and controlling what we see online with minimal regulation. We need to create new publicly owned organizations that will provide a public alternative to privately owned digital platforms, be democratically organized and run, generate pioneering digital content, develop innovative technological solutions to advance democracy and harness data for the public good. This would be the best way of safeguarding the future creative and informational needs of publics in the face of constant market encroachment into public services.

- Net neutrality legislation should be in place and enhanced and expanded to address the myriad ways in which network operators can promote or demote particular content or services based on their ability to pay.
- Regulation of political advertising should prohibit and prevent the practice of buying personal data for campaign purposes without users' knowledge or consent. New rules should be introduced, requiring that all online political advertising during official election campaign periods is sufficiently signposted. This should ensure that users are made aware that the content is part of a political campaign, as well as by whom it has been commissioned and funded. In the long term, these rules could be adapted in order to limit all online political advertising to publicly owned and regulated search.

113

- Legislation should develop and implement a new system of labelling for sources of content. The rules could be applied to both major content providers and/or intermediaries. They should be designed to maximize the transparency of branded, sponsored or 'advertorial' content especially in news and information. They should also be designed with a view to promoting sources of content that are subject either to public service regulation or independent press regulation.
- Data-driven analysis and prediction should be focused on systems rather than people, and should be used to hold power to account rather than to sort populations, profile and punish the poor. This requires drawing up 'red lines' for the use of data and AI in contexts where people's livelihoods, dignity and rights will be significantly impacted.

These requirements are the minimal benchmarks for ensuring and protecting a plural, sustainable and diverse media and communications ecology that can contribute to a healthy democracy. Without the above reforms, our media will become ever more concentrated in ever fewer hands, yet more susceptible to market pressures and distorted by commercial priorities and be increasingly less diverse in every way.

Crucially, in our focus on democratic intent, we must bring the public back into the equation. In carrying out our diagnosis, we need to change the composition of the decision-making table in a way that privileges community and citizen voices, particularly those who have been most discriminated against: the already resource-poor and marginalized. The turn to data can serve as an avenue for questioning our decision-making processes in contemporary democracy at large. We are already seeing this with the rise of citizen juries and assemblies that have all been used for questions of data collection, particularly in the public sector in the UK. In the United States, the American Civil Liberties Union has successfully helped establish community oversight bodies in various cities to oversee any acquisition of surveillance technologies by the police. In Barcelona, we are seeing experiments with a more radical response to surveillance capitalism that tries to honour publicly owned and citizen-centred data infrastructures with comprehensive community oversight. Although flawed and compromised, these are all part of a growing appetite for bottom-up democracy that privileges citizen voices.

In order to advance this appetite for bringing

democratic purposes back into the fray, a concern with media and data justice goes beyond individual privacy and the protection of personal data and cannot rely simply on policy and regulation. Instead, claiming media and data justice needs to be rooted in organizing solidarity networks and building on historical struggles over the distribution and recognition of public goods, rights and freedoms. We have seen the power of communities in pushing back against the might of media moguls and the logic of data accumulation, both individually and collectively, through various forms of legal challenge, whistleblowing, pressure group campaigning and social movements for media reform. All these activities are focused on directing resources away from oppressive media and data systems that are hell-bent on profit towards investing in structures that nurture the democratic health and vitality of communities.

This manifesto for media reform is a call to communities and social movements, to trade unionists and to citizens, to students and scholars, to seek out the means of claiming media and data justice. We believe that this has to be premised on a socialist politics that can advance freedom, equality, collectivism and ecological sustainability, while avoiding corporate, financial and market domination. Critically, we need to imagine data and media systems that prioritize the value of the public over profit, and collaboration over competitiveness and to develop economies that go beyond capital. Operationally, this means that we have to formulate mechanisms of inclusive citizen participation and democratic control of the spaces we inhabit. Rethinking and rebuilding our media and data worlds according to these principles will require enormous energy and enthusiasm. We will have to learn from other social struggles and solidarity movements that have sought to advance economic equality, civil rights and social justice; but we do so on the basis that there can be no meaningful democracy without media reform and data justice.

Notes

1 Challenging Media Power Today

1 Quoted in a transcript of a meeting of Ogilvy staff obtained by BuzzFeed News (2019), 21 July, https://www.buzzfeednews.com/article/lamvo/ogilvy-transcript-meeting-customs-border-seifert-immigration

2 Quoted in Paul Bond (2016) 'Leslie Moonves on Donald Trump: "It May Not Be Good for America, but It's Damn Good for CBS"'. *Hollywood Reporter*, 29 February. https://www.hollywoodreporter.com/news/leslie-moonves-donald-trump-may-871464

3 Richard Waters (2019) 'Google Parent Alphabet Overtakes Apple to Become New King of Cash'. *Financial Times*, 31 July. https://www.ft.com/content/332dd974-b349-11e9-8cb2-799a3a8cf37b

4 Bernie Sanders (2019) 'Op-Ed: Bernie Sanders on his Plan for Journalism'. *Columbia Journalism Review*, 26 August 2019. https://www.cjr.org/opinion/bernie-sanders-media-silicon-valley.php

5 Pierre Bourdieu (1991) *Language and Symbolic Power*. Cambridge: Polity, p. 166.
6 See Des Freedman (2014) *The Contradictions of Media Power*. London: Bloomsbury.
7 Quoted in Freedman (2014), p. 89.
8 Henry Jenkins, Sam Ford and Joshua Green (2013) *Spreadable Media: Creating Value and Meaning in a Networked Culture*. New York: NYU Press.
9 Andrew Chadwick (2017) *The Hybrid Media System: Politics and Power*. Oxford: Oxford University Press, 2nd edn), p. 21.
10 Michel Foucault (1977) *Discipline and Punish: The Birth of The Prison*. London: Vintage, p. 174.
11 Michael Foucault (1980) *Power/Knowledge: Selected Interviews and Other Writings*. London: Pantheon, p. 156
12 See Michael Foucault (2002) *Power,* vol. 3 of *The Essential Works of Foucault*. London: Penguin, 2002 for a comprehensive range of readings on Foucault's conception of power.
13 See, for example, Shoshina Zuboff (2019) *The Age of Surveillance Capitalism*. London: Profile, in which she develops the concept of 'instrumentarian power' and argues that it is 'in the nature of instrumentarian power to operate remotely and more in stealth. It does not grow through terror, murder, the suspension of democratic institutions, massacre or expulsion. Instead it grows through declaration, self-authorization, rhetorical misdirection, euphemism, and the quaint, audacious backstage moves

specifically crafted to elude awareness.' For a power-ful critique of Zuboff's book, which suggests that she is tougher on surveillance than she is on capital-ism, see Evgeny Morozov (2019) 'Capitalism's New Clothes'. *The Baffler*, 4 February. https://thebaffler. com/latest/capitalisms-new-clothes-morozov

14 Karl Marx (1852) *The 18th Brumaire of Louis Bonaparte.* https://www.marxists.org/archive/marx/ works/1852/18th-brumaire/ch07.htm

15 See Siva Vaidhyanathan (2018) *Anti-Social Media*. Oxford: Oxford University Press.

16 *E-Marketer* (2019) 'Facebook and Google Control Ever-Greater Portion of UK Ad Market', 26 March. https://www.emarketer.com/content/facebook-and-google-control-ever-greater-portion-of-uk-ad-mark et; Felix Richter (2019) 'Infographic: The Incredible Size of Google's Advertising Business', *International Business Times*, 22 August. https://www.ibtimes. com/infographic-incredible-size-googles-advertising-business-2816856

17 Martin Moore and Damian Tambini (2018) 'Conclusion' in Moore and Tambini (eds) *Digital Dominance*. Oxford: Oxford University Press, p. 398.

18 See Benjamin Birkinbine, Rodrigo Gomez and Janet Wasko (eds) (2017) *Global Media Giants*. London: Routledge, for a comprehensive overview.

19 Anna Nicolaou (2019) 'A Second Wave of Media M&A is Coming'. *Financial Times*, 7 August. https:// www.ft.com/content/9629af48-b8b3-11e9-8a88-aa 6628ac896c

20 See the comprehensive list of country reports on media concentration at http://www.mom-rsf.org

21 See, for example, the report of the Cairncross Review (2019) *A Sustainable Future for Journalism*, 12 February. https://assets.publishing.service.gov.uk/go vernment/uploads/system/uploads/attachment_data/ file/779882/021919_DCMS_Cairncross_Review_.pdf

22 Quoted in Jane Martinson (2016) 'Did the *Mail* and *Sun* help swing the UK towards Brexit?', *Guardian*, 24 June. https://www.theguardian.com/media/2016/ jun/24/mail-sun-uk-brexit-newspapers

23 Justin Schlosberg (2018) 'Digital Agenda Setting: Reexamining the Role of Platform Monopolies' in Moore and Tambini, *Digital Dominance*, p. 214.

24 See the Media Reform Coalition's 2019 report, *Who Owns the UK Media?* https://www.mediareform.org. uk/wp-content/uploads/2019/03/FINALonline2.pdf.

25 Stephen Cushion et al. (2018) 'Newspapers, Impartiality and Television News', *Journalism Studies* 19(2): 171–8.

26 Eugenia Sipera et al. (2018) 'Refugees and Network Publics on Twitter: Networked Framing, Affect and Capture', *Social Media and Society*. https://doi.org/ 10.1177/2056305118764437

27 See *Who Owns the UK Media?* and Ofcom's *News Consumption in the UK 2018*, https://www.ofcom. org.uk/__data/assets/pdf_file/0024/116529/news-con sumption-2018.pdf

28 Laura Basu (2018) *Media Amnesia: Rewriting the Economic Crisis*. London: Pluto, p. 24.

29 Mike Berry (2019) *The Media, The Public and the*

Great Financial Crisis. London: Palgrave Macmillan, pp. 277–8.

30 See Al Jazeera (2018) 'Why Media Need to Turn Up the Temperature on Climate Change', 22 October. https://www.aljazeera.com/programmes/listeningpost/2018/10/media-turn-temperature-climate-change-181020140721880.html

31 Media Matters for America (2019) 'Majority of Top Newspapers in Agricultural Producing States Fail to Mention UN Climate and Land Report on Their Front Pages', 14 August. https://www.aljazeera.com/programmes/listeningpost/2018/10/media-turn-temperature-climate-change-181020140721880.html

32 See Des Freedman (2018) 'Corbyn Framed and Unframed' in Mark Perryman (ed.), *The Corbyn Effect*. London: Lawrence and Wishart, pp. 96–111.

33 See various chapters in Dan Jackson et al. (eds) (2019) *Election Analysis 2019*, Centre for the Study of Journalism, Culture and Community. http://www.electionanalysis.uk

34 Sutton Trust (2019) *Elitist Britain 2019*. https://www.suttontrust.com/research-paper/elitist-britain-2019/, pp. 37–8.

35 See Berry (2016) *The Media, The Public and the Great Financial Crisis;* Justin Schlosberg, 'Should He Stay or Should He Go? Television and Online News Coverage of the Labour Party in Crisis'. Media Reform Coalition. https://www.mediareform.org.uk/wp-content/uploads/2016/07/Corbynresearch.pdf

36 Owen Bennett-Jones (2018) 'Can't Afford to Tell the Truth'. *London Review of Books* 40(24): 32.

37 See Shoshana Zuboff (2019) *Surveillance Capitalism: The Fight for a Human Future at the New Frontier of Power*. London: Profile; Nick Couldry and Ulises Mejias (2019) *The Costs of Connection*. Stanford: Stanford University Press; Moore and Tambini (2018) *Digital Dominance*; Victor Pickard (2019) *Democracy without Journalism: Confronting the Misinformation Society*. Oxford: Oxford University Press.

2 Claiming Media Justice

1 See 'Introduction' in D. Freedman, J. A. Obar, C. Martens and R. W. McChensey (eds) (2016) *Strategies for Media Reform: International Perspectives*. Fordham: Fordham University Press.

2 See B. Chapman (2018) 'Google Must be Broken up to Save News Media – says Rupert Murdoch's News Corp'. *Independent*, 12 March. https://www.independent.co.uk/news/business/news/google-news-corp-rupert-murdoch-australia-break-up-monopoly-competition-a8819501.html

3 See, for instance, V. Pickard (2016) 'Yellow Journalism, Orange President'. *Jacobin*, 25 November. https://www.jacobinmag.com/2016/11/media-advertising-news-radio-trump-tv/

4 P. McNally (2008) 'Emily Bell Predicts Two Years of Media Carnage'. *Press Gazette*, 15 October. https://www.jacobinmag.com/2016/11/media-advertising-news-radio-trump-tv/

5 J. Kucharczyk (2013) 'Ancillary Copyright in

Germany: From Opt-Out to Opt-In on Google News'. *Disco (Disruptive Competition Project).* http://www. project-disco.org/intellectual-property/070113-ancill ary-copyright-in-germany-from-opt-out-to-opt-in-o n-google-news/#.Vobi5fmLSM_

6 See, for instance, P. Napoli and R. Caplan (2017) 'Why Media Companies Insist They're not Media Companies, Why They're Wrong, and Why it Matters'. *First Monday*, 22(5).

7 J. Schlosberg (2013) 'Coopting the Discourse of Crisis: Reassessing Market Failure in the Local News Sector' in J. Mair, R. L. Keeble and N. Fowler (eds) *What Do We Mean by Local?* London: Abramis Academic Publishing.

8 See P. Norris (2000) *A Virtuous Circle: Political Communications in Post-Industrial Societies.* Cambridge: Cambridge University Press.

9 J. Waterson (2019) 'Guardian Breaks Even Helped by Success of Supporter Strategy'. *Guardian*, 1 May. https://www.theguardian.com/media/2019/may/01/ guardian-breaks-even-helped-by-success-of-support er-strategy

10 F. Cairncross (2019) 'Cairncross Review: A Sustainable Future for Journalism', p. 14. https://assets.publish ing.service.gov.uk/government/uploads/system/uploa ds/attachment_data/file/779882/021919_DCMS_Ca irncross_Review_.pdf

11 A. McSmith (2012) 'Revealed: Murdoch's Secret Meeting with Mrs Thatcher Before he Bought *The Times*'. *Independent*, 17 March. http://www.indep endent.co.uk/news/media/press/revealed-murdochs

-secret-meeting-with-mrs-thatcher-before-he-bought
-the-times-7575910.html

12 See M. Curtiss, K. A. Bharat and M. Schmitt (2014).
    Patent Indentifier No. US 2014/0188859 A1. United
    States: Google.com

13 P. Brown (2018) 'Study: Apple News's Human
    Editors Prefer a Few Major Newsrooms'. *Tow
    Center*, 5 June. https://www.cjr.org/tow_center/stu
    dy-apple-newss-human-editors-prefer-a-few-major-n
    ewsrooms.php

14 M. Nunez (2016) 'Want to Know what Facebook
    Really Thinks of Journalists? Here's what Happened
    when it Hired Some'. *Gizmodo*, 3 May. https://www.
    cjr.org/tow_center/study-apple-newss-human-edito
    rs-prefer-a-few-major-newsrooms.php

15 See Communications and Markets Authority (2018)
    'A Report on the Anticipated Acquisition by 21st
    Century Fox, Inc of Sky Plc', 1 May. https://assets.
    publishing.service.gov.uk/government/uploads/sys
    tem/uploads/attachment_data/file/713920/CMAFox
    Sky_report_nonconfidential.pdf

16 E. Nechushtai and S. C. Lewis (2019) 'What Kind
    of News Gatekeepers do we Want Machines to be?
    Filter Bubbles, Fragmentation, and the Normative
    Dimensions of Algorithmic Recommendations'.
    Computers in Human Behavior, 90, p. 298.

17 See, for instance, R. A. Harder, J. Sevenans and P.
    Van Aelst (2017) 'Intermedia Agenda Setting in the
    Social Media Age: How Traditional Players Dominate
    the News Agenda in Election Times'. *International
    Journal of Press/Politics*, 22(3): 275–93.

18 J. M. Yun (2019) 'News Media Cartels are Bad News for Consumers'. *Competition Policy International's North American Column* (April).

19 M. Taibbi (2019) 'Youtube, Facebook Purges are More Extensive than You May Think'. *Rolling Stone*, 7 June. https://www.rollingstone.com/politics/politics-features/youtube-facebook-purges-journalists-845790/

20 Among the Council's largest funding sources in 2018 were the US, UK and UAE governments – see 'Honor Roll of Contributors', *Atlantic Council*. https://www.atlanticcouncil.org/support-the-council/honor-roll-of-contributors/

21 See Taibbi (2019).

22 D. Wakabayashi (2017) 'As Google Fights Fake News, Voices on the Margins Raise Alarm'. *New York Times*, 26 September. https://www.nytimes.com/2017/09/26/technology/google-search-bias-claims.html

23 J. Daniels (2018) 'The Algorithmic Rise of the "Alt-Right"'. *Contexts* 17(1): 60–5.

24 J. Schlosberg (2016) *Media Ownership and Agenda Control: The Hidden Limits of the Information Age*. London: Routledge.

25 R. J. Pingree, A. M. Quenette, J. M. Tchernev and T. Dickinson (2013) 'Effects of Media Criticism on Gatekeeping Trust and Implications for Agenda Setting'. *Journal of Communication*, 63(2): 351–72.

26 J. Gottfried, M. Barthel and A. Mitchell (2017) 'Trump, Clinton Voters Divided in Their Main Source for Election News'. *Pew Research Center*, 18

January. https://www.journalism.org/2017/01/18/tr
ump-clinton-voters-divided-in-their-main-source-fo
r-election-news/

27 Pew Research Center (2018) 'An Examination of
the 2016 Electorate, Based on Validated Voters', 9
August. https://www.people-press.org/2018/08/09/
an-examination-of-the-2016-electorate-based-on-val
idated-voters/

28 See S. Tien (2018) 'Top Twitter Demographics that
Matter to Social Media Marketers'. *Hootsuite*, 26
June. https://blog.hootsuite.com/twitter-demographi
cs/

29 See S. Perlberg and M. Di Stefano (2017) 'Rupert
Murdoch is the Media's Unlikely Hero in the War
Against Google and Facebook'. *Buzzfeed* (4 October).
https://www.buzzfeednews.com/article/stevenperlbe
rg/rupert-murdoch-is-the-medias-unlikely-hero-agai
nst-tech

30 W. L. Bennett and S. Livingston (2018) 'The
Disinformation Order: Disruptive Communication
and the Decline of Democratic Institutions'. *European
Journal of Communication*, 33(2): 122–39.

31 Bennett and Livingston (2018).

32 Bennett and Livingston (2018: 128).

33 Gottfried et al. (2017).

34 Gottfried et al. (2017).

35 See N. Confessore and K. Yourish (2016) '$2 Billion
Worth of Free Media for Donald Trump'. *New
York Times*. https://www.nytimes.com/2016/03/16/
upshot/measuring-donald-trumps-mammoth-advant
age-in-free-media.html

36 T. Patterson (2015) 'News Coverage of the 2016 General Election: How the Press Failed Voters'. *Shorenstein Center on Media, Politics and Public Policy.* https://shorensteincenter.org/news-coverage-2016-general-election/

37 G. Greenwald (2019) 'Robert Mueller did not Merely Reject the Trump–Russia Conspiracy Theories. He Obliterated Them'. *The Intercept.* https://theinter cept.com/2019/04/18/robert-mueller-did-not-mere ly-reject-the-trumprussia-conspiracy-theories-he-obl iterated-them/

38 See, for instance, J. Schlosberg and L. Laker (2018) 'Labour, Antisemitism and the News: A Disinformation Paradigm'. Media Reform Coalition. https://www.mediareform.org.uk/wp-content/uplo ads/2018/09/Labour-antisemitism-and-the-news-FI NAL-PROOFED.pdf

39 R. Tait, L. Harding, E. MacAskill and B. Quinn (2018) 'No Evidence Corbyn was a Communist Spy, Say Intelligence Experts'. *Guardian,* 20 February. https://www.theguardian.com/politics/2018/feb/20/ no-evidence-corbyn-was-spy-for-czechoslovakia-say-intelligence-experts

40 E. Lucas (2018) 'Jeremy Corbyn's Sickening Support of Soviet Empire'. *The Times*, 22 February. https://www.thetimes.co.uk/article/corbyn-s-sickeni ng-support-of-soviet-empire-qcpgs70gg [behind pay-wall]

41 See P. McKeigue, D. Miller, J. Mason and P. Robinson (2018) 'Briefing Note on the Integrity Initiative'. *Working Group on Syria, Propaganda and Media,*

21 December. http://syriapropagandamedia.org/
working-papers/briefing-note-on-the-integrity-initia
tive

42 J. Ferguson (2018) 'Secret Scottish-Based Office Led
Infowars Attack on Labour and Jeremy Corbyn'.
Sunday Mail, 9 December. https://www.dailyrecord.
co.uk/news/politics/foreign-office-funds-2m-infow
ars-13707574

43 As per the UK's system of 'press recognition' established in the wake of the phone hacking scandal and
based on the recommendations of B. Leveson (2012)
'An Inquiry into the Culture, Practices and Ethics of
the Press: Report'. https://assets.publishing.service.
gov.uk/government/uploads/system/uploads/attachm
ent_data/file/270939/0780_i.pdf

44 See C. Tobitt (2019) 'Left-Wing Website the
Canary most Complained about Impress-Regulated
Publication of 2017/18'. *Press Gazette*, 10 January.
https://pressgazette.co.uk/left-wing-website-the-can
ary-most-complained-about-impress-regulated-publi
cation-of-2017-18/

45 Pickard (2016).

46 B. Cathcart and P. French (2019) 'Unmasked: Andrew
Norfolk, *The Times* Newspaper and anti-Muslim
Reporting'. Media Reform Coalition. <https://www.
mediareform.org.uk/wp-content/uploads/2019/06/
Norfolk_Report-FINAL.pdf

47 E. Shugerman (2017) 'Sexual Harassment Costs
Fox News up to $110 Million in last Nine Months'.
Independent, 11 May. https://www.independent.
co.uk/news/world/americas/fox-news-sexual-haras

sment-cases-payouts-settlements-bill-o-reilly-roger-a
iles-a7730556.html
48 Bennett and Livingston (2018: 128).

3 Advancing Data Justice

1 S. Zuboff (2019) *The Age of Surveillance Capitalism*. London: Profile Books.
2 E. Morozov (2019) 'Capitalism's New Clothes'. *The Baffler*, 4 February. https://thebaffler.com/latest/capi talisms-new-clothes-morozov
3 N. Couldry and U. Mejias (2018) 'Data Colonialism: Rethinking Big Data's Relation to the Contemporary Subject'. *Television and New Media*, 20(4): 338.
4 S. Zuboff (2015) 'Big Other: Surveillance Capitalism and the Prospect of an Information Civilization'. *Journal of Information Technology*, 30(1): 75–89.
5 A. McStay (2018) *Emotional AI: The Rise of Empathic Media*. London: Sage.
6 J. Van Dijck (2014) 'Datafication, Dataism and Dataveillance: Big Data Between Scientific Paradigm and Ideology'. *Surveillance and Society*, 12(2): 199.
7 B. E. Harcourt (2015) *Exposed: Desire and Disobedience in the Digital Age*. Cambridge, MA: Harvard University Press.
8 M. Andrejevic (2019) 'Automating Surveillance'. *Surveillance and Society*, 17(1/2): 7–13.
9 D. Lyon (2015) *Surveillance after Snowden*. Cambridge: Polity.
10 A. Hintz, L. Dencik and K. Wahl-Jorgensen (2018)

Digital Citizenship in a Datafied Society. Cambridge: Polity.

11 V. Eubanks (2018) *Automating Inequality: How High-Tech Tools Profile, Police, and Punish the Poor*. St Martin's Press.

12 K. Yeung (2018). 'Algorithmic Governance: Towards a New Public Analytics?' *Paper given at THINKBIG Workshop*, Cumberland Lodge, 25 June.

13 L. Dencik, J. Redden A. Hintz and H. Warne (2019) 'The '"Golden View": Data-Driven Governance in the Scoring Society'. *Internet Policy Review*, 8(2): DOI: 10.14763/2019.2.1413

14 J. Sadowski (2019) 'When Data is Capital: Datafication, Accumulation, and Extraction'. *Big Data and Society*. January–June 2019: 1–12.

15 M. Poon (2016) 'Corporate Capitalism and the Growing Power of Big Data: Review Essay'. *Science, Technology and Human Values,* 41(6): 1088–1108.

16 L. Amoore (2013) *The Politics of Possibility: Risk and Security Beyond Probability*. Durham and London: Duke University Press.

17 Andrejevic (2019) as above.

18 N. Couldry (2015) 'The Myth of "US": Digital Networks, Political Change and the Production of Collectivity'. *Information, Communication and Society*, 18(6): 608–26.

19 Hintz, Dencik and Wahl-Jorgensen (2018) as above.

20 V. Bakir et al. (2015) 'Public Feeling on Privacy, Security and Surveillance'. A Report by DATA-PSST and DCSS. https://mappedsites.cardiff.ac.uk/dcssproject/wp-content/uploads/sites/24/2015/11/

Public-Feeling-on-Privacy-Security-Surveillance-DA TAPSST-DCSS-Nov2015.pdf; L. Rainie (2018) 'Americans' Complicated Feelings about Social Media in an Era of Privacy Concerns'. *Pew Research Center*, 27 March. https://www.pewresearch.org/fa ct-tank/2018/03/27/americans-complicated-feelings-about-social-media-in-an-era-of-privacy-concerns/

21 N. Draper and J. Turow (2019) 'The Corporate Cultivation of Digital Resignation'. *New Media and Society*, 21(8): 1824–39.

22 L. Dencik (2018) 'Surveillance Realism and the Politics of Imagination: Is there no Alternative?' *Krisis: Journal for Contemporary Philosophy* (1): 31–43.

23 D. McQuillan (2019) 'AI Realism and Structural Alternatives'. Paper given at Data Justice Lab Workshop, Cardiff University. http://danmcquillan. io/ai_realism.html

24 H. Kennedy, D. Elgesem and C. Miguel (2015) 'On Fairness: User Perspectives on Social Media Data Mining'. *Convergence: The International Journal of Research into New Media Technologies*, 23(3): 270–88; A. Smith (2018) 'Public Attitudes Toward Computer Algorithms'. *Pew Research Center*. https:// www.pewinternet.org/2018/11/16/public-attitudes-toward-computer-algorithms/

25 O. Williams (2019) 'How Big Tech Funds the Debate on AI Ethics'. *New Statesman*, 6 June. https://www. newstatesman.com/science-tech/technology/2019/ 06/how-big-tech-funds-debate-ai-ethics

26 J. Naughton (2019) 'Are Big Tech's Efforts to Show

it Cares About Data Ethics Another Diversion?'
Guardian, 7 April: https://www.theguardian.com/
commentisfree/2019/apr/07/big-tech-data-ethics-div
ersion-google-advisory-council

27 O. Solon and S. Siddiqui (2017) 'Forget Wall
Street – Silicon Valley is the new Political Power in
Washington'. *Guardian*, 3 September. https://www.
theguardian.com/technology/2017/sep/03/silicon-
valley-politics-lobbying-washington

28 L. Stark and A. L. Hoffman (2019) 'Data is the
New What? Popular Metaphors and Professional
Ethics in Emerging Data Culture'. *Journal of
Cultural Analytics*. DOI: 10.31235/osf.io/2xguw; L.
Taylor and L. Dencik (forthcoming) 'Constructing
Commercial Data Ethics'. *Regulation and
Technology*.

29 B. Wagner (2018) 'Ethics as an Escape from
Regulation: From 'Ethics-Washing' to Ethics-
Shopping?' In E. Bayamlioglu, I. Baraliuc, L. A. W.
Janssens and M. Hildebrandt (eds) *Being Profiled,
Cogitas Ergo Sum*. Amsterdam: Amsterdam
University Press, pp. 84-90.

30 Nora Zelevansky (2019) 'The Big Business of
Unconscious Bias'. *New York Times*, November.
https://www.nytimes.com/2019/11/20/style/diversi
ty-consultants. html. For information about FAT*
events, see: https://www.fatml.org/

31 L. Dencik, F. Jansen and P. Metcalfe (2018) A
Conceptual Framework for Approaching Social
Justice in an Age of Datafication'. *Working Paper,*
DATAJUSTICE project. https://datajusticeproject.

net/2018/08/30/a-conceptual-framework-for-appro aching-social-justice-in-an-age-of-datafication/

32 M. Cyril (2009) 'Media Justice: Out of the Margins'. *FAIR*, 1 May. https://fair.org/extra/media-justice-out-of-the-margins/

33 S. P. Gangadharan and J. Niklas (2019) 'Decentering Technology in Discourse on Discrimination'. *Information, Communication and Society*, 22(7): 882–99.

34 J. Buolamwini and T. Gebru (2018) 'Gender Shades: Intersectional Accuracy Disparities in Commercial Gender Classification'. *Proceedings of Machine Learning Research*, 81: 1–15.

35 S. Noble (2018) *Algorithms of Oppression*. New York: New York University Press.

36 M. Burgess (2018) 'Facial Recognition Tech used by UK Police is Making a Ton of Mistakes. *Wired*, May 4. https://www.wired.co.uk/article/face-recognition-police-uk-south-wales-met-notting-hill-carnival

37 R. Benjamin (2019) *Race After Technology*. Cambridge: Polity.

38 R. Crooks (2019) 'What We Mean When We Say #AbolishBigData2019'. *Medium*, 22 March. https://medium.com/@rncrooks/what-we-mean-when-we-say-abolishbigdata2019-d030799ab22e

39 B. Tarnoff (2019) 'To Decarbonize We Must Decomputerize: Why We Need a Luddite Revolution'. *Guardian*, 18 September. https://www.theguardian.com/technology/2019/sep/17/tech-climate-change-luddites-data

4 *Articulating a Politics of Hope*

1 See Sara Banet Weiser (2018) *Empowered: Popular Feminism and Popular Misogyny*, Durham: Duke University Press for a discussion of how the digital age is seeing a surge of misogyny. See also Jack Bratich and Sarah Banet-Weiser (2018) 'From Pick-Up Artists to Incels: Con(fidence) Games, Networked Mysogyny and the Failure of Neoliberalism'. *International Journal of Communication* 13(19): 5003–27.

2 See Media Reform Coalition (2018) 'Submission to Cairncross Review'. London: MRC. https://www.mediareform.org.uk/get-involved/mrc-submission-to-cairncross-review.

3 See for example: Oxfam (2019) *Public Good or Private Wealth?* London: Oxfam GB; J. Cribbs, A. N. Keiller, and T. Waters (2018) *Living Standards, Poverty and Inequality in the UK: 2018*. London: IFS; Danny Dorling (2014) *Inequality and the 1%*. London: Verso.

4 See S. Armstrong (2018) *The New Poverty*. London: Verso.

5 See Armstrong (2018) above and T. Piketty (2014) *Capital in the Twenty-First Century*. Harvard University Press.

6 See the damning report by the IPPC (2018) *Global Warming of 1.5°C, an IPCC Special Report on the Impacts of Global Warming of 1.5°C above Pre-Industrial Levels and Related Global Greenhouse Gas Emission Pathways, in the Context of Strengthening the Global Response to the Threat*

of Climate Change, Sustainable Development, and Efforts to Eradicate Poverty. Korea: IPCC. http://www.ipcc.ch/report/sr15/

7 Wendy Brown (2015) *Undoing the Demos: Neoliberalism's Stealth Revolution*. Cambridge, MA: MIT Press.

8 Grace Blakeley (2019) *Stolen: How to Save the World from Financialization*. London: Repcater Press.

9 The Edelman Trust Barometer surveys over 33,000 people in 28 countries across the globe. In 2018, when asked to indicate which institution they trusted to do what is right, 'the media in general' came out as the least trusted institution in 22 of the 28 countries. 63 per cent of people globally said that the average person does not know how to tell rumour from falsehoods. The same survey also revealed that 33 per cent of people are reading or listening to the news less and 19 per cent are avoiding the news altogether because it's too depressing (40%); too one-sided or biased (33%) or controlled by hidden agendas (27%). 66% of people said that news organizations were more concerned with attracting a big audience than reporting.

10 See D. G. Blanchflower (2019) *Not Working: Where Have All the Good Jobs Gone?* New Jersey: Princeton University Press.

11 Prominent reports in the UK have observed that the need to seek the voice of marginalized and disadvantaged people in decision-making processes is of acute local, national and global relevance. See RSA (2017) *Citizenship 4.0: An Invitation to Power Change* and

CSF (2018) *Civil Society in England: Its Current State and Future Possibilities.*

12 Brian Leveson (2012) *The Leveson Inquiry: The Report into the Culture, Practices and Ethics of the Press.* London: The Stationery Office.

13 See Natalie Fenton (2018) 'Regulation is Freedom: Phone Hacking, Press Regulation and the Leveson Inquiry – The Story So Far'. *Communications Law* 23: 3.

14 Natalie Fenton was vice chair of the board of directors of Hacked Off (2012–18), the campaign group established in the wake of the hacking scandal, whose aim was to bring about a fair, accountable and effective system of independent press regulation. See Natalie Fenton (2018) 'The Scandalous Power of the Press: Phone Hacking in the UK' in H. Tumber and S. Waisbord (eds) *Routledge Companion to Media Scandal.* London: Routledge.

15 For example, see Ben Birkinbine (2018) 'Commons Praxis: Towards a Critical Political Economy of the Digital Commons'. *tripleC* 16(1): 290–305; G. De Peuter and N. Dyer-Witheford (2010) 'Commons and Cooperatives'. *Affinities: A Journal of Radical Theory, Culture, and Action* 4(1): 30–56.

16 Alternative Models of Ownership, Labour.org.uk, 2018.

17 These have been adapted from Nancy Fraser's three normative criteria for evaluating emancipatory possibilities as set out in Nancy Fraser and Rahel Jaeggi (2018) *Capitalism: A Conversation in Critical Theory.* Cambridge: Polity.

18 Des Freedman (2018) '"Public Service" and the Journalism Crisis: Is the BBC the Answer?' *Television and New Media*, 20(3): 203–18.

19 Tom Mills (2016) *The BBC: Myth of a Public Service*. London: Verso and the Media Reform Coalition (2019) *Media Manifesto 2019*. https://www.mediar eform.org.uk/blog/media-manifesto-2019

20 See R. Davies, A. Haldane, M. Nielsen and S. Pezzini (2014) 'Measuring the Costs of Short-Termism'. *Journal of Financial Stability*, 12: 16–25.

21 See Ben Birkinbine (2018) 'Commons Praxis: Towards a Critical Political Economy of the Digital Commons'. *tripleC* 16(1): 290–305.

22 On a research project investigating the news needs of local communities Fenton et al. proposed the idea of a local news hub that could be shared between radio, print and TV news journalists and be a site of community engagement and media training befitting the notion of a media commons. See Natalie Fenton, Monika Metykova, Justin Schlosberg and Des Freedman (2010) *Meeting the News Needs of Local Communities*. London: The Media Trust.

23 In general there are five types of cooperatives: worker cooperatives, consumer cooperatives, purchasing cooperatives, producer cooperatives and multi-stake holder cooperatives. For more detail see http//www.iwdc.coop/why-a-coop/five-types-of-cooperatives-1

24 See Trebor Scholz and Nathan Schneider (2016) *Ours to Hack and to Own: The Rise of Platform Cooperativism*. New York: OR Books.

25 Media Reform Coalition (2017) *Mapping Changes in*

Local News: More Bad News for Democracy. http://www.mediareform.org.uk/wp-content/uploads/2017/12/mapping-changes-in-local-news-2015-2017-interactive-research-report-march-2017.pdf

26 See A. Gabbatt (2018) 'New Jersey Pledges $5m for Local Journalism to Boost State's "Civic Health"'. *Guardian*, 6 July. https://www.theguardian.com/us-news/2018/jul/06/new-jersey-journalism-local-news-civic-information-consortium

27 Erik Olin Wright (2010) *Envisioning Real Utopias*. New York: Verso.

5 Conclusion: A Manifesto for Media Reform

1 Hancher, L. and Moran, M. (1989). *Capitalism, Culture and Economic Regulation*. Oxford: Clarendon Press.

2 We would like to acknowledge some of the key sources of inspiration for this chapter: Charlotte Ryan, *Prime Time Activism: Media Strategies for Grassroots Organizing*. South End Press, 1990; Jeremy Corbyn, 'Alternative MacTaggart Lecture', 23 August 2018; Leo Watkins, 'Democratising British Journalism: A Response to Jeremy Corbyn's Alternative MacTaggart Lecture'. *New Socialist*, 12 September 2018; Justin Schlosberg (2018) 'Mission of Media in an Age of Monopoly'. *Res Publica*, 26 May; Dan Hind and Tom Mills (2018) 'Media Democracy in openDemocracy'. *New Thinking for the British Economy*, 2018. Media Reform Coalition, *Media Manifesto 2019*.

3 A one per cent levy on the UK digital advertising revenues of Google and Facebook alone would raise in
excess of £70 million. Some countries have attempted
to address digital disruption to news publishing businesses by enforcing so-called 'ancillary' copyrights.
In 2013, the German government passed legislation
requiring digital intermediaries to obtain a licence
from publishers to include cached content from their
articles in search listings or news feeds. But a law
intended to make Google pay for the use of such 'snip-
pets', quickly became a law that forced publishers to
agree *not* to be paid. Other European countries have
pursued divergent paths in dealing with this issue. In
France, for instance, publishers agreed to lay their
claims to rest after Google promised a fund for supporting digital innovation in journalism. In Spain on
the other hand, legislators passed a much tougher
version of Germany's ancillary copyright law in
2014, making it illegal for publishers to 'opt in' and
extending copyright restrictions to cover *any* amount
of copyrighted text or hyperlinks. Google's response
in that case was simply to shut down its Spanish news
service altogether. Given the demonstrable capacity
for these monopolies to avoid corporation tax by
redirecting profits away from the jurisdictions in
which they are generated, there is both a moral and
economic rationale for a small levy on their digital
advertising revenues.

4 In the UK, the Bristol Cable set up as a Media
Co-operative and runs via a local monthly membership fee, crowd funding and grant awards. The

Ferret, also a co-operative run by its members and funded by subscriptions, donations, paid-for stories or material and grants, gains its following from being democratic and having a clear public purpose. Far more organizations could attract grant funding if journalism in the public interest was recognized as a charitable purpose in the UK. Unless such possibilities are legislated for, the danger is that news organizations turn to branded-content and native advertising that threatens to damage trust in news still further. Or, they continue to rely on unpaid labour that ultimately will reduce the sustainability and quality over time.

5 Research by Schweizer et al. (2014) on fourteen European media systems, the US, Canada, New Zealand and Australia noted that policy-makers can support private media organizations with tax relief or direct subsidies to specific media companies (including online media) without compromising media independence if safeguards such as statutory eligibility criteria are in place. They point out that some countries, including those who consistently score highly on the Press Freedom Indices, have long and successful traditions of supporting the press. General measures (such as some form of tax relief, or reduced tariffs of telecommunications, electricity, paper or transport; or subsidies for news agencies, journalism, schools, etc.) do not prevent media ownership concentration, while selective measures can help weaker media organizations. Direct press subsidies are used in several countries, either to maintain struggling

news organizations to preserve media diversity and pluralism (e.g. Canada, France, Denmark, Netherlands) through a distribution aid, export aid, support for the internal training of journalists, or the formation and re-organization of newspapers; or to support newspapers in minority languages (Finland). The authors conclude that their comparison of 18 media systems indicates that where there is political will to support news organizations and journalism, policy-makers can choose from an array of options with established methods for ensuring editorial independence and that 'direct production support to selected economically struggling media based on clear criteria is most suitable to help maintaining plurality and editorial competition' (p. 14).

6 Julia Cagé (2020) *The Price of Democracy: How Money Shapes Politics and What to Do About it*, Harvard University Press, also discusses the democratic merits of a voucher system for funding the media.